This book is dedicated

In Loving Memory to my Daughter

Margaret "Peggy" Ellis Campbell
Peg o' my Heart

And to my children and grandchildren

Leslie Ellis Sharbel
John Howard Ellis
Margaret Carolyn Sharbel
Arthur John Sharbel, IV
Charles Truman Sharbel
John Hardin Ellis
William Boland Ellis

Who are the last known living descendants of
Tobias Francis Boland

THE IRISH PIONEER

A Historical Novel

Based on the life of
Tobias F. Boland

The Irish Pioneer: Tobias Boland

A Historical Novel
by
Margaret Boland Ellis
and
Thomas L. Rooney

ISBN-0-9759397-5-0
978-0-9759397-5-8

As a historical novel, the events and central characters of this work are based on actual people, facts, and events of history. To make the story more enjoyable, literary license has been taken with some of the lesser characters and with day to day events, feelings, and emotions expressed by the people in the novel.

Cover Design by Carolyn Miller Design
Cover Image by Carl Rakeman, Courtesy of
Department of Transportation/Federal Highway Administration

Printed in the United States

Magnolia Mansions Press
Mobile, Alabama
www.magnoliamansionspress.com

PROLOGUE

This historical novel is a story based on the life of my great-grandfather, Tobias Francis (Tobey) Boland, a pioneer from Tipperary, Ireland, who came to the United States of America in the early eighteen hundreds, landing in New York. He was a contractor and a builder of canals, railroads, churches, schools and a college. Although he had a number of children, I am the only living member of my generation, and only my three children and their five children continue this Boland line. I hope this telling will provide a new interest in Tobey Boland and will be appreciated by those seeking to follow family histories. I also trust the citizens of Worcester, Massachusetts, where Tobias Boland lived many years of his life, will come to recognize him as the founding pioneer that he was. He lived in Boston as well where he spent many years planning and building churches, including the Cathedral of the Holy Cross which he did not live to see completed.

I am indebted to Thomas Rooney of Shrewsbury, Massachusetts, who provided large amounts of previously unknown data. Mr. Rooney has kindly contributed information and edited this manuscript for historical accuracy. His editorial comments have been invaluable.

I knew something of Tobey from items sent to me when the old residence on Hollywood Street in Worcester was sold in the seventies. Thomas Rooney spurred my interest by sending many clippings and books with details about Tobey Boland as the contractor for the Blackstone Canal. The canal runs from Worcester, Massachusetts, to Providence, Rhode Island; it was completed in 1828 by Tobey and his Irish workers not long after he arrived in this country.

Mr. Rooney has written and published a children's illustrated book called ***Tobey Boland and the Blackstone Canal***. He is presently active in historical societies in Shrewsbury and often gives talks about the building of the Blackstone Canal and The College of the Holy Cross and other significant happenings in the history of Worcester and surrounding area.

A historian must write from real history, but as a historical novelist, I have elected to enlarge that information writing of the actions, feelings, and emotions of these early pioneers. And thus I attempt to make great-grandfather Tobias Boland, his family and those around him more than a list of historical facts, but living human beings.

Here, then, is the story of Tobias Francis Boland, the Irish Pioneer.

Margaret Boland Ellis
June 1, 2009

CHAPTER ONE

Two Irishmen stood overlooking the Hudson River, which flowed below their stand on the platform at the end of the newly completed Erie Canal. Sunlight reflected on the river below sending sparkling rays across the area where the canal waters joined the river for the first time. The date was October 26, 1825, a glorious autumn day with a light breeze blowing across the banks of the river and over the large crowd who waited for the arrival of the first barge ever to come down this new and much anticipated waterway called the Erie Canal. Shipping goods by water instead of the slow overland method was expected to bring much prosperity to New York State and the port of New York City. This venture would open the young United States to the vast western regions beyond the Appalachian Mountains.

The larger of the two men was Tobias Francis Boland, a tall muscular fellow who stood more than six feet. He had a thick head of red hair, and a full copper-colored beard, and sky blue-colored eyes. Tobias had arrived in the United States only a few months earlier. The second man was Philip Naughton, brother-in-law of Tobias. These two had been working on the construction of canals for several years prior to 1825 both in Ireland and England, and each had contributed to the final stages of the Erie Canal.

Philip turned to Tobey and said, "Governor DeWitt Clinton should be here soon to dedicate this project. He has worked hard to see it accomplished."

"He wouldn't miss this occasion. From what we've heard, it took his strong leadership and political connections to get a job of this magnitude passed by the state legislature," Tobias said.

"Yes," Philip said, "Governor Clinton deserves the credit and the honor of dedicating this magnificent example of engineering."

"I'm glad to be here for the celebration of the opening of the Erie Canal, even if I didn't get here in time to do much work on it," Tobias said.

"True enough. It's exciting to be here, and I'm glad to have you with me because without your willing cooperation, I couldn't have been here myself in time to work on any of the building of this canal. And because of this work, I now understand much better what basic knowledge is involved in constructing a canal of this magnitude. I regret you could not get here for the whole process, but I can teach you the things I've learned so you will be able to supervise building a canal on your own. I've seen and learned enough that will benefit us handsomely, especially you, Tobey, for I predict that one day you will become one of the outstanding contractors in this whole new United States of America. You have the natural ability, the youth and the strength to accomplish this. There is already talk about other canals to be built, including one between Massachusetts and Rhode Island. We must look into that one as soon as possible."

"I hope I can live up to your expectations," the young man said. "Without your guidance and you and my sister taking me into your family when you did, there would be no chance for me to be where I am today."

Tobias Francis Boland was the son of John and Mollie Blake Boland, who had married later in life after the deaths of their first spouses. Tobey was born of this union on January 7, 1795, but he soon lost both of his parents. His mother died first, and shortly thereafter his father was killed in a stable accident.

Tobey's older sister, Mary, and her husband, Philip Naughton, had taken the orphaned lad into their home after the death of John Boland. Any other solution was too horrible to contemplate. Ireland was a very poor country at that time, and there was little work to be had. Most Irishmen tended small farms and had heavy payments to English landlords. A boy like Tobey would have been hard pressed to get enough food to eat or a place to lay his head had his sister and her husband not taken him in.

Philip Naughton was a builder and a contractor and he recognized the strength and determination in Tobey, who was eager to pay his way in exchange for the generosity of the couple. Tobey was soon a strapping youth, an early bloomer who was big and strong and willing to work. In later years he often thought how different his life might have been had he been thrown into the world of the early nineteenth century and had to struggle on his own. Tobey was a cooperative young man and Philip utilized his size and strength and put him to work at construction jobs. As he began to teach Tobey knowledge of the building trade, Philip also realized the young man had a natural aptitude for construction and had many good ideas to make progress and save time and money on various jobs.

Philip was a man of vision, and one day, after study and careful thought, told Tobey they were going to

England where there were many more jobs building canals and even talk of railroad construction.

"There's not enough construction here in Ireland for us builders," Philip told Tobey. "With little but farming the Irish economy is not likely to support much else at the present time. Ireland is home and a wonderful country, but it is not going to play a significant part in this Industrial Revolution that is fast coming to Europe. England is using the latest methods for building canals for transportation, and they have so many future plans to build railroads. If we are going to succeed in our chosen line of work and make enough money to provide a comfortable living for ourselves and our families, we have to go where the work is and learn the newest techniques. I want you to become the best contractor you can possibly be, and England is the place to learn what you need to know."

Shortly after this conversation, Tobey and Philip left for England. The thought of leaving the Ireland he loved was disturbing to Tobey, but he put his trust in Philip and was willing to follow him wherever Philip thought the work and learning was to be found.

Tobey did his best to hide the choking tears he felt forming in his eyes as he and Philip said good bye to Mary and to the green hills of Ireland and set out across the sea to England. Tobey loved his sister Mary, who had become a mother to him. She and Philip were the only family he had. He hugged Mary tightly for a long time until she stepped back and said, "Ah, Tobey, little brother, you must not be sad. 'Tis the thing you must do this leaving Ireland with my Philip. But you must always remember the land of your birth. And never forget that to be Irish is to know that in the end, the world will break your heart."

Tobey would remember those words for the rest of his life.

In England the bond grew between Philip and Tobey as strong as true blood brothers. As Philip had anticipated, the two of them soon found there were many job openings in the building of canals for skilled laborers as they were. Philip saw to it that Tobey was always on the same jobs as he was so that he could protect his young brother-in-law. Tobey continued to grow in stature, and he worked hard and learned quickly. When he did not understand a procedure, he asked questions. He was good at solving problems about construction methods. Tobey used his strength to undertake any job no matter how long or difficult. He was also now large enough and tough enough to take care of himself among the work crews engaged in this hard and difficult work. Fights often broke out, and Tobey would defend himself and also Philip. Tobey was now a head taller than his mentor and much stronger and more muscular. His size and attitude earned Tobey the respect of the gangs and the bosses of the projects. His good judgment and talent as a peacemaker were not overlooked either.

Philip was always on the lookout for more construction jobs and new and interesting building projects. One day he and Tobey learned that America was planning to build the biggest canal in the world in New York State.

"We have to go to America," Philip said, "For it is there that we find a new land of opportunity. We've learned about all we can in England. America is a new country and the opportunities there are unlimited."

"Will we take Mary with us?" Tobey asked. "We can't leave her alone in Ireland much longer."

"Of course we'll take Mary. We'll go back to Tipperary and get her and then sail from Cork. This job in England is nearly finished. We can head for America by way of Ireland. We've made enough money here for our sea passage and lodging once we arrive in New York. You have the wisdom to see, as I do, that future work here in England is limited when compared to the vast openings that will be available in the new United States. I have no doubt they will build that large canal in the state of New York. Robert Fulton, that fellow who has developed the wonderful new steam engine power, wrote to the New York Governor DeWitt Clinton, from London back in 1797, urging the construction of a canal from Lake Erie to the Hudson River. And it has been proposed by the governor of the state of New York, and the idea tossed about in the legislatures with some representatives favoring it and others very much opposed to it. Governor Clinton kept lobbying to get the project moving. Those opposed to digging such a canal called it 'Clinton's Big Ditch'. Even President Thomas Jefferson did not favor the idea, though from what I can gather, he is a very intelligent man and progressive as well. But after talk of constructing such a canal was discussed for many years, now it appears the Erie Canal has actually begun. It will run from Buffalo, New York, on Lake Erie east to the Hudson River around Albany, New York. That's three hundred sixty-three miles through very wild and fierce country.

Governor Clinton has already turned the first shovel of dirt on July 4, 1817. We must get to America. We are late already."

Tobey had great confidence in Philip Naughton's judgment and was receptive to any suggestion from his brother-in-law. The two men planned to travel to the United States of America as soon as possible.

But this was not so easy. Their plans were shattered when the head contractor of their present job refused to release them until all work was completely finished on the canal where they were presently working. He stated he would not pay the two men if they left early.

Philip argued that he needed to go to Ireland to see to the sale of his property there, and he finally persuaded the job boss to change his mind. Philip could leave, but Tobey would have to remain in England as a project supervisor until all work was finished on the canal and the waterway opened for traffic.

Once again, Philip came up with still another plan. "I'll go to Ireland and get Mary," he said, "And she and I will leave for America as soon as we can sell our property and arrange passage for an Atlantic crossing. We will set up living quarters in New York, and I can apply for work on the Erie Canal. As soon as you finish here, you will have enough money to book passage directly to New York and you can join us there."

And so Philip soon left, and Tobey threw himself into finishing the work, pressing his crew to expedite the construction. The days passed and eventually the construction was completed. Tobey even received a small bonus for his leadership and early completion of the canal. He hastened to take a coach to Liverpool where he boarded the first available ship, *The Young Phoenix*, to the United States of America. Tobey was never to see England or Ireland again.

One reason Tobey never again returned to the British Isles was his tendency to seasickness. The ocean trip across the North Atlantic by sailboat usually took five to six weeks depending on the winds and the weather. The first week at sea Tobey spent most of the time lying in his bunk. Other passengers were seasick and still others had various other illnesses, some life threatening. Several passengers were ailing with what was called "ship sickness," others had tuberculosis. Two died and had to be buried at sea. There were times when Tobey was so miserable he contemplated jumping overboard—anything to stop the up and down and side to side motion of the ship.

Tobey was not able to eat and began to lose weight as well as feel miserable almost all the time. Finally one of the ship mates took pity on him and gave him some bread and rum, and Tobey was able to survive. No one was happier than Tobey to see the shores of America as the ship and sailed along Long Island and then up the harbor to dock at a wharf at the port city of New York.

The Young Phoenix sailed into port early in January 1825 and Tobey was ever so glad to put his feet on solid ground again. The weeks that the voyage had taken seemed more like years. Philip, who had checked for the arrival of ships, soon came to the pier to welcome Tobey when he had debarked and cleared the immigration station.

"It has been such a long time since we were last together," Philip said. "You've arrived just as work is finishing up on the construction of the Erie Canal, but you can go with me for the final work and be present for the opening celebration. Governor Clinton is going to board the first barge in Buffalo and with the other dignitaries will ride the length of the canal and hold an opening ceremony near Albany about the end of October. You and I will have time to go see the engineering work of the canal as I finish my assignment there."

"When do we leave?" Tobey asked.

"We'll overnight at the inn where Mary and I are staying, but then you and I have to leave. I've arranged for us to take a boat up the Hudson River to Albany. Water travel is quicker--one more reason why the Erie Canal will be an improvement in passenger travel as well as freight movement. New York City is bound to be one of the most important seaports in the country—bigger than Boston or even New Orleans in the South at the mouth of the great Mississippi River. I have some final inspections of some of the locks as you accompany me on this trip. The engineering marvel is probably the most advanced work ever done in this country. The new trade route to the west will mean prosperity to that region as well. It will soon be possible to ship goods down the Erie Canal to the Hudson River and New York and then right on to Europe."

Tobey was excited and eager to see the canal. "The Erie Canal has to be the engineering marvel of the day," he said. "I can't imagine eighty-three locks and a rise of five hundred sixty-eight feet from the Hudson

River to Lake Erie. And you say it is only four feet deep though it is forty feet wide."

"Just wait," Philip smiled. "You are not going to believe the wonder of the Erie Canal until you actually see it."

CHAPTER TWO

The whirlwind ride by stage coach from the port of New York to the inn where Philip and Mary Naughton were temporarily residing was filled with new sights for the young Irishman. As the carriage rolled along the streets of New York, Tobey marveled at the buildings and their size. More construction was going on everywhere. Tobey was so glad to be on the solid earth and, after the weeks of fasting on the ship, he was finally very hungry. Seeing Mary again brought joy to his heart for he loved his older sister dearly and had missed her terribly. Philip had become a father figure as well as brother-in-law, business partner, and best friend.

The inn provided a fine meal that evening and Tobey was happy he could eat again. Philip had wisely decided that Tobey should have a bit of rest and a night's sleep on dry land. He and Tobey would leave early the next day to journey to the site of the Erie Canal at Albany. For the first time in many nights, without the rolling of the ship, Tobey slept soundly.

The sun was just rising when the two men left the inn and proceeded to the wharf where a flat barge was loading cargo and passengers for the trip north up the Hudson River. The trip would take all day, and Tobey was relieved to learn the motion of the barge was nothing like that of an ocean vessel so he was able to enjoy the trip without the agony of sea sickness.

"The most practical way for us to move along the canal and conduct my final inspections is to go by horseback," Philip explained. "I've arranged for us to rent some good trail horses for our trip. That way you can see up close the details of the canal and its construction. We'll stay at work camps along the way since I am hired on the Erie Canal staff until the dedication ceremony and a bit longer to assure everything is running smoothly. Not only will this be an orientation trip for you, but with your help, I will be able to complete all my tests and make my reports."

Tobey stood forward on the deck of the barge and ate an apple that had been provided by the inn for their traveling lunch. He marveled at the Hudson River and studied how it provided a passage to the north and also south to the open seas which he had so recently and thankfully vacated. He could imagine how the new canal would open traffic of goods to be shipped from the western parts of the new country to the port of New York and on to points all over the world.

"When he leaves for the initial trip from Buffalo to Hudson River at Albany, we calculate it will take Governor Clinton eleven days. He'll make stops along the way to make speeches and for political contacts and assure everything is in order for the flow of traffic which will begin to move both ways on the Erie Canal. Meantime, we have a couple of months to finish up my inspection. I think I can arrange for you to do some work as well. Then you can always say you worked on the Erie Canal. That could be helpful in the future."

After the barge had tied up at their destination and the two Irishmen had left the boat and secured their trail horses, they rode along the banks of the Erie Canal where Philip pointed out and explained its many engineering aspects. As always, Tobey was fascinated with the construction and absorbed every piece of information Philip provided and carefully stored it in his mind for future use.

"There are eighteen aqueducts to carry the canal over the ravine and rivers as I have told you," Philip said. "And the eighty-three locks handle the rise of five hundred sixty-eight feet from the Hudson to Lake Erie. It's amazing that the forty-foot wide trench is only four feet deep, but still the floated boats will be able to carry up to thirty tons of freight. This ten-foot wide towpath we ride on now will accommodate horses, mules and oxen led by the boat drivers or "hoggees" as they are called. The canal is already getting a reputation and songs have been created about it. You'll hear some of them sung in the camps as we move along the canal."

"This is the longest by far of any other canal ever built in Europe or America isn't it?" Tobey asked.

"Yes, and this big ditch Clinton fought so hard to get goes right through the downtown area of Rochester," Philip said. "We'll spend several nights there. I want to introduce you to an engineer named Benjamin Wright if we can find him. He has handled most of the construction of the middle portion of the Erie. He is a brilliant engineer."

Tobey took in every detail and asked hundreds of questions about construction and such parts as the culvert, the formations called the piers, and of course the locks. They could hear some of the workers singing the songs Philip had mentioned. As they sat by the light of the camp fire, Philip explained technical methods and uses of procedures and drew rough illustrations which Tobey carefully saved and put in his knapsack.

As they rode along one morning, Tobey said to Philip. "As wonderful as this Erie Canal is, it is only going to be of use until railroads are built. Just before I left England the British were finishing the Stockton and Darlington Railroad, and they will begin work on the construction of a railroad between Liverpool and Manchester by 1830. The invention of the steam engine will make all the difference in transportation."

Philip listened carefully and smiled. "I've never doubted your foresight, Tobey, and I think this time you will be right about the railroads taking over. But my boy, I want you to be able to build them all—canals, railroads, churches and schools. Being a contractor will provide you with a comfortable living, and you will be doing a great service to this new country."

The time riding along the canal working and inspecting passed quickly and Tobey continued to observe and keep his notes on everything he saw and all the things Philip told him. His notebook was being filled with details of construction.

And now, the day had arrived when the two men stood with the crowd gathered to greet Clinton's barge ***The Seneca Chief*** as it arrived. Tobey and Philip and the rest of the crowd which had gathered waited for the governor's arrival and his declaration that the Erie Canal was open for business.

A cheer went up as the governor's barge came in sight. The vessel drifted near and was met by a crew of men who secured it to the wharf. Governor Clinton stepped forward from the rest of the crowd on the barge and proceeded to the bow of the boat. In his arms he held a large keg.

"In this keg, I have brought water from Lake Erie," he said, and stepped to the edge of the deck. Lifting the keg high above his head, he poured the water from the keg into the Hudson River.

"I declare the Erie Canal open for shipping," Clinton said above the roar of the crowd. A band struck up "Hail Columbia" and flags waved.

Tobey looked at Philip and drew his mouth into a tight line. "The next time a canal is opened," Tobey said, "It is going to be one that I have built."

"I don't doubt it a bit," Philip said and slapped Tobey on the back.

CHAPTER THREE

After the excitement of the Erie Canal opening, the trip back down the Hudson River was anti-climatic. Conversation among the passengers on board was political, with much speculation about the election of Andrew Jackson as new president of the United States. Tobey was too new in the country to know about the government. He thought he would learn soon enough as he began to conduct business in his new home land.

The thought of seeing his sister Mary again and being with her and Philip gave him much to look forward to. Tobey spent his hours on the down river barge looking over his notes and asking Philip for further explanations of the engineering techniques.

After the three of them were reunited, Philip, Tobey and Mary were to remain in New York at the inn only a short time. The two men had barely rested from their physical work at the canal site and their travel when Philip announced they were moving to Washington, D.C.

"Washington is the fast-growing seat of the new government of the United States," Philip said. "It is in that city where we will find the opportunity to learn of and to secure much new construction business."

"The men on the barge said the new capital city is pretty much a swamp area," Tobey said.

"Yes, I heard that, too. But George Washington picked the site in 1791, and it is one of the few places in the world where the city is being laid out before anything is built. Washington engaged a Frenchman named Pierre L'Enfant to design the streets and avenues and the plan is unique. They had already started the Capitol Building and the residence for the presidents, and some other government buildings, but then the War of 1812 with the British came along. A lot of the new city was burned by the English in 1814. We'll actually go to Georgetown to live. It's an older and more settled community where most of the social activity of the area takes place. The Jesuits have a large community there, and Georgetown is next door to Washington where the government activities take place and where new contracts will be let."

The Naughtons and Tobey left New York City by stage coach and found temporary quarters in Georgetown. As he always was when encountering new sights and places, Tobey was fascinated with the hustle and bustle of the growing city of Washington. When he did not accompany Philip on business seeking trips, Tobey set out on long walks about the area. He was especially interested in the restoration of the White House where the presidents were to reside. It had suffered damage during the 1812 war while President John Adams was the first presidential occupant. He listened with great interest about Adams' wife, Abigail, taking the large portrait of George Washington to safe keeping when the attack was near. He heard other talk of the plans for the Capitol building.

And, among other things, he also discovered that the Baptist Church on the corner down from the rooming house where they had established temporary residence, held gatherings every Saturday night in their activities building next door to the church. There were lots of free refreshments, music, singing, and even some folk dancing, which surprised the Irishman as he had heard the Baptists held very different beliefs from those of his Catholic upbringing. Although Tobey's mother, Mollie Blake Boland had been a member of the Church of Ireland, which was really the Anglican Church of England, she had subscribed to the Catholic faith of her husband, John Boland. Though both parents had died when he was very young, the Catholic Church was the only one Tobey had ever known. He had not gone to any services in a long time, as attending Mass was not easy when on construction jobs. Tobey never considered any other religion–in fact he rarely thought of spiritual things or of faith.

Philip continued to seek new projects, proposals and contracts and any chance to secure more employment in the building fields. Some days Tobey went with him, but mostly, Toby was left on his own to explore Washington.

And so on Saturday evenings, Tobey began to regularly attend the gatherings at the Baptist Center. There he found other young people his own age, and for the first time in his life, he had a social life with his peers and he thoroughly enjoyed this new activity.

One night Tobey met a charming and beautiful young woman named Mary Ellen McCauley. She was the daughter of a physician who also served as a Baptist minister at the church which sponsored the Saturday night gatherings. Tobey thought Mary Ellen was the most beautiful girl he had ever seen. It was true that in his busy life of construction jobs, he had little time to meet any girls let alone spend any time in female company. He at first was timid and awkward about approaching and talking to her; but Mary Ellen, who showed interest in the tall handsome Irishman with the red hair, soon put Tobey at ease. Except for the times when she had to attend to duties as one of the hostesses, she and Tobey spent entire evenings together, talking, laughing, and dancing. Mary Ellen impressed Tobey as very intelligent, charming, and more educated than other women he had known, though that number was quite small.

Tobey taught Mary Ellen some of the few traditional Irish steps that he knew, but he liked it best when they danced a waltz and he could hold her closer to him. He felt he could look into her sparkling eyes and dance forever.

"I think our Tobey fancies the young lady at the Baptist parties," Mary Naughton said to her husband Philip one day as they were having a Sunday meal at the boarding house where they were still living.

Tobey felt his face burning and he knew it must be turning red. "She's a lovely lass," was all Tobey could think to say, but he didn't deny his feelings for Mary Ellen.

Mary just smiled and the meal continued.

"We can't live in this boarding house much longer," Philip said. "We need a home of our own. I am looking to see what is available."

As Tobey heard that, an upsetting thought came to him. If they moved far away, he might not get to the Saturday night events and that meant not seeing Mary Ellen. It had become very important for him to see her.

He had not anticipated either that he and Philip would make a trip to Baltimore to do consulting about building in that area. But Philip announced they must go, and on Saturday night Tobey had to tell Mary Ellen he was accompanying his brother in-law on this business trip. Tears came to her eyes and Mary Ellen said she would miss him. She urged him to come to her home as soon as he returned to Washington.

While in Baltimore, Tobey and Philip chanced to meet Benjamin Wright again. He was the engineer they had seen briefly during the Erie Canal work in Rochester.

"If you fellows are looking for more canal work, I have a bit of news," Wright said as they sat at an evening meal.

"We're always ready to find new construction," Tobey said with interest. "Tell us about it."

Wright began the explanation with some background. "This venture is called the Blackstone Canal. The idea has been around since 1792 when John Brown, a ship owner and entrepreneur, proposed building a canal from Providence, Rhode Island, through Massachusetts. He had a grand idea of running it through New Hampshire and Vermont, connecting to the Connecticut River and on into New York. Rhode Island accepted and endorsed the concept, but the 1796 Massachusetts State Legislature in Boston saw this as an economic threat to Boston and defeated the legislation.

"The idea came up again in 1817 when work on the first section of the Erie Canal was begun. The whole nation supported the beginning of that operation, and the Blackstone Canal idea once again came before the legislature of both Rhode Island and Massachusetts. This time both states' legislatures have voted favorably to dig such a canal."

Wright continued, "Actual work should have started about 1822 when I helped draw up the plans and specifications. However, digging did not begin until 1826, and the results were disastrous. My survey was not followed. The original contractor used farm boys who knew nothing about building canals. The walls of his canal caved in and the firm handling the contract lost more than $100,000.

"That part of the Blackstone will have to be rebuilt. It will take a contractor who knows what he is doing to direct the repair work and set right the rest of the canal digging. They would have two such men with you, Philip, and Tobias here."

"Are there enough construction workers besides the farm boys available in that area?" Tobey asked.

"There should be by now," Wright answered. "We have brought some of the workers over from the Erie Canal, now that it is finished and in operation. And you two will be interested to know that Irish workers are currently being recruited. The Irish fellows are more experienced at canal work and the recruits are beginning to arrive in the United States. It is anticipated that there will be at least one thousand skilled Irish canal builders available to work on the Blackstone Canal by 1827."

On the bouncing coach ride back to Washington, the Blackstone Canal was the main topic of conversation between Philip and Tobey. "It's a great opportunity," Philip said. "We must take the necessary steps to be in line to get that contract."

Back in Georgetown, as soon as he had properly greeted his sister Mary, Tobey excused himself and went immediately to the home of Mary Ellen

McCauley. He had never been to her home, which was next door to the church. He had seen her only at the Saturday night gatherings, but Tobey had thought of her constantly and missed her greatly while in Baltimore. And, after all, she had invited him to call as soon as he got back to Georgetown.

He was eager to discuss his travels and learn what she had been doing in his absence. He hoped she had not made any new gentlemen friends. Really, he just wanted to see her as he had determined she was the woman he wanted to marry. Would she accept him? Would her father allow him to marry an Irishman? He thought of such things as he walked to the McCauley house. Unless he could take her with him as his wife, she was the one reason he was not eager to go to Rhode Island and Massachusetts should the Blackstone Canal job open up. He decided not to mention the fact that he might be leaving for a long period of time. At least not right now.

Tobey was startled when he was greeted at the door by Mary Ellen's father, a large man with a full bushy beard and head of thick black hair. He had a full mustache that spread across the bottom of his face. The Reverend Doctor McCauley, as tall as Tobey, eyed Tobias Boland from head to foot. He did not smile.

"What is it you want young man?" he asked sternly.

"Good day to you, sir," Tobey said. "God bless all here in this house."

"And what is it that you want?"

"I, er, well, sir, I have come to see your daughter, Mary Ellen."

"It is a bit unusual to call at this hour of the day without a proper appointment,"

"Yes, sir, but you see, sir, I have been away on a business trip, and I haven't seen Miss McCauley for such a long time. She asked me to let her know when I was back in town, and I didn't want to wait till the Saturday night meeting to see her."

"And what business is it that you are in that takes you traveling?" McCauley had not stepped back and he was still barring the doorway.

"I'm a builder, sir, and a contractor." Tobey stood his ground. "I have worked on the Erie Canal and other large projects."

Tobey looked over McCauley's shoulder and saw Mary Ellen in the hall way behind her father. When the young woman saw Tobey, she let out a scream of delight.

"Oh, Father," she said and she rushed to the door. "It's my friend Tobey Boland. Do let him come in. I haven't seen him for such a long time. I thought he was gone forever."

Still studying Tobey again with obvious doubt, the reverend doctor slowly stepped aside. "Come into the parlor then, young man, but mind your manners and ask first before you come to our house calling again."

"Yes, I will do that, sir," Tobey said, "Thank you." He stepped through the doorway and followed the reverend doctor and Mary Ellen.

The three advanced to the parlor and Mary Ellen sat down on the sofa. Her father followed the couple and motioned for Tobey to sit in a chair across the room. He then sat beside his daughter. There was an awkward pause in conversation and silence hung heavy in the air.

"Tell us about your trip to Baltimore," Mary Ellen said.

"My brother-in-law, Philip Naughton, and I went to Baltimore to investigate contracts for any kind of building available. We have worked on canals in England and on the Erie Canal in this country, as I have told you." He looked at McCauley.

"Aren't you a bit young to call yourself a contractor?" the minister asked.

"It may seem so," Tobey said. "But I began to work with Philip in Ireland when I was very young, and with my brother-in-law, I have experience in the building trade in England before coming to the United States."

"And so you are Irish and that would mean you are a Papist." McCauley said. Tobey saw a frown cross his face. Tobey had never before been called a Papist, and wasn't really sure what it meant other than it was a word he'd heard applied to Catholics. He decided it must be a term used in America.

"I was born into the Catholic faith if that is what you mean, sir," Tobey said.

"Nearly all you Irishmen are," Dr. McCauley said.

"Oh, Father, what difference does that make? Mary Ellen smiled at Tobey. "We can still be friends."

Mary Ellen's father did not acknowledge her remarks and made no attempt to leave the room. Instead he asked Tobey many more questions about his work in the building profession. When the noon meal was announced, Mary Ellen looked at her father with pleading eyes and asked if Tobey could stay for the meal.

After a long pause her father took a deep breath and then agreed. "It's highly unusual," he said, "Even though your manners did not dictate that you schedule a call at our home, we can show that we are well bred and have you join us for the noon meal. I would like to continue to discuss the construction work you do."

Tobey was glad for the time with Mary Ellen, but he had a suspicious feeling during the entire meal that Mary Ellen's parents were studying him to determine if he was properly qualified to spend any more time with their daughter. He wondered if they were going to allow a Papist in their midst. Did he dare bring up marriage?

The next day Philip told Tobey they would leave the following day for Rhode Island and the hearing for awarding the contract for the Blackstone Canal. They were to travel up the Atlantic coast by boat. The very idea of a sea voyage made Tobey feel sick, but that feeling was nothing like the way his heart sank at the idea of leaving Mary Ellen. He knew he had to go. He owed it to Philip, and building was his livelihood. Philip said an overland trip by coach would take too long. Time was of the essence if they were to get the job of building the Blackstone Canal.

He went to Mary Ellen's house to tell her the news that he must leave Washington again. Just when he was accepted to call on the McCauleys, and he thought he would have time to strengthen their relationship, he would have to leave. He had no idea when he would ever see her again. There was nothing to do but ask her to marry him and wait for his return.

Once again tears came to Mary Ellen's eyes when Tobey told her he was leaving Washington for Rhode Island and Massachusetts and that he did not know when he might return.

"Will you wait for me, Mary Ellen?" he asked. "I will be back as soon as I can, and if I get the contract for the Blackstone Canal, I will have the money for us to get married. I shall ask your father for your hand in marriage, that is, if you will have me."

"You want me to be your wife?" Mary Ellen smiled and bowed her head.

"More than anything in the world," Tobey said. He took her hand in his. "I want to ask Dr. McCauley right now."

"He isn't here," Mary Ellen said. "You will have to come back tonight and ask him."

Tobey had to argue with Philip about going back to the McCauleys to speak to the doctor. Philip was quiet for a while after Tobey told him his plans.

"It's not a good time to be marrying," he said. "We can't delay our trip. And you will be gone for many months, could be even years, on the canal job if we get it. Will this young lady be willing to wait that long for you?"

"She says she will wait," Tobey said, "and I believe her, so let me go to their house tonight and get her father's permission before we leave."

Tobey was not prepared for the reaction of the Reverend Doctor, who fumed at Tobey when he asked for the hand of his daughter.

"Of course you cannot marry my daughter," he roared. "I will not consent to her marrying a foreigner, let alone an Irish Catholic, and living the life of a traveling builder of whatever it is you do, constructing canals, buildings, roads. What kind of life would that be? No, I will not give my consent even if you should offer to give up your Papist ways and become an American citizen and a Baptist. In fact you would have to be a Baptist before I would ever even think of allowing such a marriage."

Dr. McCauley was so angry that Tobey did not know what to say. He sighed and finally said, "Could I at least tell her good bye?"

Dr. McCauley thought a long time and finally said, "Very well. I guess I can allow that. It will probably be the last time you ever see her."

He turned and walked quickly away, bumping into Mary Ellen in the hall where she had apparently been listening to her father's shouting.

She fell into Tobey's arms and burst into tears. "I don't care what he says," she said. "I want to be your wife, and I will wait forever for you to come back."

"I will be back. You can trust me on that. Then we will change his mind," Tobey said. "If I get this job, I will have lots of money. I will be a good husband." Tobey paused and took a deep breath. "To have you for my wife, I will even join the Baptist church if that is what it takes to change your father's mind."

With a sad heart, Tobey left Mary Ellen, who stood on the front porch and waved goodbye to him. Tobey looked back and waved. He shook with anger and frustration. He fought down the catch in his throat, and realized he now knew what his sister had meant when she told him:

To be Irish is to know that in the end, the world will break your heart.

CHAPTER FOUR

Once again Philip and Tobey were traveling. While on the journey, which took several weeks, Philip broke the news to Tobey that he would recommend him, his protégée, to be appointed chief builder on the Blackstone. Philip said he would be returning to Washington for work on a government building that had just been awarded to him.

Philip said they would soon meet with Benjamin Wright again when they got to Providence. Wright should have finalized work on the surveying for the route. Philip said he thought Wright would agree to recommend Tobey for the portion of the canal from Worcester, Massachusetts to Rhode Island.

"If you are determined to be married, this canal will put you in the position of a successful contractor and you can return and get your Mary Ellen."

Tobey knew he could build canals even if it meant carving through hills and primitive forests. He thought he could control the tough and restless Irish workers. But the thought of doing such a job without Philip nearby was challenging. He could do it. He would do it–if and when he got the contract.

To his great relief Tobey found travel on the boat up the Atlantic coast was not as difficult as his North Atlantic voyage. The time was much shorter and the seas seemed to be less violent nearer the coast. Maybe he was getting his sea legs, he thought. He was none the less glad to put his feet on solid and dry land again.

A delegation awaited them in Providence. Benjamin Wright, Chief Engineer of the middle section of the Erie Canal, and his assistant Holmes

Hutchinson were there as expected, along with the committee of investigation.

Wright reported that his 1822 survey showed a descent of four hundred fifty-one and a half feet from Thomas Street in Worcester, Massachusetts, to the tide water at Providence, Rhode Island. He noted that approximately forty locks would be needed to raise and lower canal boats along the route and suggested locations for these locks. He also showed where water could be acquired to fill the locks and thus keep an adequate water level in both the canal and the river. He told Tobey to read his survey and note the details of how North Pond and Dority Pond in Millbury, Massachusetts, could supply the water needed. Wright added that the charter for the Blackstone Canal Company had been executed by the Legislature of Massachusetts back in March of 1823 and approved by Rhode Island General Assembly in June of 1823.

"We are a very long time getting to the completion of this canal project, and you can understand the anxiety of the committee and the stock holders to get work going immediately," Wright said.

He then addressed the present state of progress on the canal. "While some work has been done, it will all have to be rebuilt. The original contractor used local farm laborers, and they had no knowledge of how to build a canal. We have some experienced Irish laborers on hand already, and we have sent for more."

Wright paused and looked at the committee members and then toward Tobey. "It is my recommendation that Tobias Boland, here present, be contracted to go to Worcester and begin the canal southward. He not only has extensive canal building knowledge, but he is also Irish and should be able to better control and deal with the workers from his native country."

There was a polite murmur of conversation from the committee. Wright spoke further.

"I can put my men to work immediately on the repair, actually the rebuilding of the first section beginning here and heading northward. Let me go on record here and say that to repair and rebuild this Rhode Island end is going to run at least $100,000, but it must be done."

Talk immediately ensued among members of the committee and Wright waited for it to die down before continuing.

"I think we have covered what you need to know to make your decision for hiring a contractor to begin at once from Worcester south. Each day we delay beginning this work puts us further behind. When will we have your decision on Mr. Boland for the contract?"

The committee chairman stood. "We have discussed this previously and we are in agreement that Tobias Boland be contracted to begin the work from Worcester as soon as he can get his work crew to that city."

The group adjourned and Wright and Tobey returned to the inn where they were staying. They sat down to have dinner together that night.

Tobey had some questions for Benjamin Wright. "Do we agree that using part of the river for the canal route will reduce building costs in terms of labor, money and time?" he asked.

"Yes, that's right," Wright said. "However, it may cause problems in the future."

"What do you mean?" Tobey asked.

"There are many mills along this route and they also use the water, and mill owners may challenge water rights if there is not enough water for both uses. We'll let others deal with that down the road, or maybe I should say, down the canal." He laughed. "Right now our job is to build the waterway. Tobey, are you ready to head to Worcester and get started?"

"I will leave tomorrow," Tobey said.

"I am pleased to be working with you," Wright said. "There is no one else even close to your qualifications. I know you will do a fine job."

That night Tobey had trouble going to sleep. This would be the first time he had ever worked without Philip nearby, close at hand to consult. But, he thought, this is my chance to establish myself as a contractor, and if I am going to be a married man, I need a good occupation, a fine reputation, and enough money coming in to adequately take care of a wife and family.

Early the next morning Tobey said goodbye to Philip, who was returning to Washington by coach. Tobey boarded another coach for Uxbridge, about half way to Worcester, where he would begin a new chapter in his life.

CHAPTER FIVE

When he arrived in Uxbridge, he found several hundred of the Irish workers were there waiting for him. Tobey called a meeting of the work crew.

"Men," he said, "We have a large job ahead of us. We will begin in Worcester, connect ponds and rivers, and dig a canal thirty-two feet wide and three and a half feet deep that will be forty-six and a half miles long."

"That's a pretty big ditch," one of the men in the front row yelled.

"It is indeed," Tobey continued. "You will be using picks, shovels, and your hands as we dig. You will be expected to move two and a half yards of dirt by wheelbarrow each hour, and we will be working ten to twelve hours a day every day but Sunday. Your pay will be nine dollars a month."

"And yourself will be watching us and not working at all but collecting a lot more money for looking. What kind of tender will we get? Irish shamrock paper?" The man who stood in the front row stepped forward and put his face right in Tobey's. "And you expect us to be satisfied with that?"

This fellow was big and rough looking, and muscular and broad of shoulders and he had a snarl on his face.

"No one is forcing you to accept this work," Tobey said patiently, but then raised his voice to continue. "But if you work for me, you will do what I say."

"Oh yeah," the man said. "Well, I say we don't take orders from a lad who is barely out of nappies." The man pushed Tobey in the chest.

Tobey's reaction was immediate. His fist shot out and connected with the man's jaw so hard the man staggered and fell to the ground. Tobey picked him up by his shirt and landed another blow that sent the fellow reeling back into the crowd. He spread his feet and stood facing the group as if daring someone to come forward and challenge him.

There was a deadly silence from the men. The dissenter got to his feet and came forward. Tobey squared himself, tightened his fists, and prepared to fight again, but the man raised both his hands and put his palms toward Tobey.

"We will do as you say," the fellow smiled and turned to the crowd. "I say this lad is a tough redheaded Irishman who knows his business. You all will do as he says."

The man turned to Tobey and extended his hand. "The name is Callahan," he said, "Michael Callahan."

"And you would be the leader of this group of workers?" Tobey said, and returned the handshake.

"You would be right," Callahan said. "Now, when do we get started digging this ditch?"

"Let's talk about that," Tobey turned the man to stand beside him and addressed the crowd again.

"The upcoming Fourth of July is a big holiday in America. In fact this July Fourth will be the fiftieth anniversary of the signing of the Declaration of Independence, a document which led to the founding of the United States of America. I propose we start walking to Worcester from here and time our arrival for the Fourth of July 1826. When the people of Worcester see us come marching in on that big holiday, they will know the Blackstone Canal will soon be a reality and make Worcester a true seaport and a growing and successful city."

When a cheer went up from the laborers, Tobey knew he had cleared a major hurdle.

The following morning at sunrise, they began the walk to Worcester. As anticipated, the crew arrived on July Fourth, expecting to join the big celebration in progress. But when they tried to enter Worcester from Uxbridge, Tobey and his crew were met by a large group of city officials who told them not to enter or to trespass into the city of Worcester, not now and not later. The officials said Irish and Catholics would not be allowed in their city.

This attitude came as a great shock to Tobey. Had not these very people come to America to escape religious prosecution in England? And, since they themselves had been victims of intolerance, how could they have become so intolerant? He and Philip had never encountered such a problem in all their building jobs. What could Tobey do? What would Philip do?

Tobey reasoned the important thing was to start the work at once. He did not want to begin the canal job amidst controversy with Worcester town folk, so he directed his men to the east side of town, the location dictated by town officials. He instructed them to set up camp and begin work on the canal as soon as possible.

On July 18, 1826, Tobey lifted the first shovel of dirt, starting at Thomas Street, and the Irish crew began to dig southward for the Blackstone Canal.

Digging through the shale was not hard, but Tobey soon found that constructing this canal properly required not just workers, but skilled quarrymen, stone sawyers, masons, ironworkers, and carpenters. All played a vital part in digging out the bed for the water way. Tobey had the added task of identifying those craftsmen from among his group of workers. More Irishmen had arrived from work on the Erie Canal, and Tobey was glad to get the skilled workers.

Chipping and digging was slow and tedious. There was grumbling among the crews and constant fighting. Tobey was glad to have an ally in his foreman, Michael Callahan. It was all the two of them could do to keep order.

However, about the only time the bickering and fighting ceased among the crews was on Sunday, the one day which they did not work. Tobey sent inquiries for a priest to come in to say Mass, but there were no priests at all in this Puritan area. Even had they been allowed to enter the town of Worcester, there were only Protestant churches there. So Tobey set up a "dry Mass," and he himself led the service, which consisted of reading scripture and prayers. These services were most often held in the open fields and around the tent shelters.

Sunday afternoons the men engaged in wrestling and boxing bouts, which fortunately served to get some of their energy routed in a better direction than the angry confrontations. They played kick ball. Tobey wondered where they got the ball. He did not have to wonder where they got the spirits. "Jigger breaks" of whiskey and rum were part of the everyday work routine, and some traveling bootleggers always seemed to appear about the time of pay day, when many workmen squandered away much of their earnings on liquor and were often drunk by sunset.

Tobey learned that keeping order among the workmen was as big a task as digging the canal. He was well aware of the group of traveling women who always seemed to be available, but in his judgment as long as they did not interfere with the digging of the canal, he decided not to approach that subject. He expected any day for the Puritan Yankee Worcester councilmen to complain to him about these women, but either they did not know of their presence or they chose to ignore it.

Slowly the work progressed. More Irish workers arrived in New York from Ireland and were sent up to the work area. The crews connected the series of ponds and rivers through the Blackstone Valley. As the canal was being built, a tangent of the canal ran in a circle around land in the area. Tobey sealed it off and drained the water which formed a triangular portion of land which the workers had called the "island." Tobey decided to put some of the living quarters in that area.

Winter soon came and the ground was frozen, so work on the canal had to stop. Tobey used this opportunity to build some tenement houses on the triangular island in the Blackstone River. Tobey had not anticipated the arrival of so many new immigrant workers from Ireland who had brought their families. Since the town of Worcester was so hostile to their entering, a place now had to be constructed for the families to live. The area called Shanty Town, for good reason, continued to grow and soon its population numbered about a thousand.

Still another challenge arrived for Tobey, who worried constantly about living conditions being so terrible. Sanitation was deplorable and there was a lack of clean water. The camp had no doctor and winter weather increased illness and death among the Irish. Tobey hoped the new housing on the island would improve conditions, but there was much work still to be done to make more comfortable homes for the work crews and their families. Without the workers there could be no canal, and without decent housing, the workers would leave and seek work elsewhere. Too many people were dying in these dreadful conditions, and Worcester forbade the burying of the Irish dead in their cemeteries. Bodies had to be shipped to Rhode Island for burial, and Tobey resolved to buy some land for a Catholic cemetery. With this in mind, he purchased some land from a man named Newton for $75.00.

Benjamin Wright arrived one day at the work scene with news from Washington. He told Tobey that both Thomas Jefferson and John Adams had died on July 4, 1826.

"That's the day we marched into Worcester from Uxbridge," Tobey said. "I can tell you I am not happy with the town officials of Worcester. They refuse to let our people come into the village. They sent us to the east side of Worcester to set up camp and it has become Shanty Town. Unfriendly people, these New England Yankees. I've had to build better housing on the island created when we diverted some of the streams, and it looks as if I am going to have to open a store where the workers can trade for necessities. We aren't allowed to go into town even to buy supplies."

"Don't let them destroy your enthusiasm, Tobey. You're doing a good job. They'll be grateful when they realize the prosperity the canal will bring to Worcester. I am surprised to hear of their actions as most of these Worcester investors in the Blackstone Canal Company are well to do merchants and professionals—young fellows in their thirties and forties and many of them have college degrees," Wright said.

"They didn't get tolerance with their degrees," Tobey said, "There are some farmers, only a few, but even so, nearly all of the Blackstone Committee are members of the Worcester Agricultural Society, a prestigious social club rather than any helpful organization."

"You have had a difficult job, but you are handling it well. Do you have a completion date in mind yet?" Wright asked.

"Yes, in spite of all the unforeseen problems that have arisen, we will be finished with this Blackstone Canal by fall of 1828."

CHAPTER SIX

The chill of the October morning air greeted Tobias Boland and Benjamin Wright as they departed for the celebration of the opening of the Blackstone Canal. The date was October 7, 1828.

"Well, Tobey," said Wright, calling him by his nickname after their years of friendship. "Did you ever think we would see this day?"

"Oh yes," Tobey replied. He greatly admired the fifty-eight-year-old American-born man. "With an engineer like you overseeing the entire forty-six and a half miles of the Blackstone, I had no doubt we'd complete this job."

"You're too modest," Wright said. "As contractor for the section of the canal between Worcester and Uxbridge, your contributions were vastly important."

"And now with a waterway from Narragansett Bay to Worcester, we can call this town a seaport, inland though it may be, miles from the ocean."

Tobey signaled their driver, Terry O'Shea, newly arrived from Ireland and a worker on the canal, that they should turn on to Summer Street. With skilled hands, Terry guided the two big stallions drawing the carriage. Manes and tails of the horses were tied with bright red ribbons.

The riders passed a newly opened country store.

"Is that your place?" Wright asked.

"Yes," Tobey replied. "We're just getting started stocking the items we need. As I promised, I opened this store for the Irish workers and their families. My crews who did such a good job on the canal work couldn't find any place to shop. I've told you before how poorly our Irish workers have been treated and that we haven't been received at all by these Yankee Puritans. As they dictated, we have settled over on the east side of Worcester in Pine Meadow, the location you know is now called Shanty Town, and with good reason. We have erected some housing for the men with families on that newly-formed island that formed when we made those water exchanges and drained the area."

Wright looked at Tobey. "If you got that fancy outfit you're wearing at your store, I'll have to pay you a visit," He smiled and tapped Tobey on the shoulder.

"You'll be welcomed," Tobey said and then looked pensive. "Not only are the citizens of Worcester shutting us out, but the merchants and mill owners along the canal are growing hostile. They act as if they own the water in the Blackstone Canal and every other tributary in the state."

"We talked about that once before if you remember," Ben said. "This morning is going to be a good test of mingling with the wealthy residents from the west side of Worcester and the work crews who have made this Blackstone Canal possible. I'm pleased that I was able to get Father Robert Woodley to come up from Rhode Island as you requested and say a Mass last week for the canal workers. They've done good work and they deserved that."

As the team of horses drew near the decorated platform, Tobey and Benjamin Wright could see the colorful bunting draped along the railings of the bandstand and around the platform and the podium located at the center of the stage. Tobey directed his carriage driver to swing around the corner to the Thomas Street dock and to prepare for a long wait.

"Looks like all 3,650 of the population of Worcester have come to see the show," Tobey said, and took a deep breath and leaned back in his carriage seat.

"We will have a while to wait," Wright said. "I don't see any sign of *The Lady Carrington* yet."

"We can sit here. They won't dare ask us to move." Toby looked around. "I personally think they should have asked us to sit on the welcoming platform. However, it's in keeping with their overall attitude. They won't admit it, but none of them would be here if it weren't for us."

"Not being appreciated is part of being in the building and engineering trade," Wright said with a smile. "After a while you get used to it. But while we're sitting here, why don't you tell me more of how you, a young man such as yourself, got in this business? We haven't had time for personal talk since that day you and Naughton came up the Hudson River to meet me and work on the Erie Canal."

"It's a long story," Tobey said.

"I think we're going to have lots of time; *The Lady Carrington* left Providence yesterday and you know it can only make about a mile and a half per hour." Wright said.

"My ship landed in New York in 1825," Tobey began. "I was so excited to be coming to this country with a new beginning and the hope of my life's work before me. That wouldn't have happened had it not been for my brother-in-law, Philip. I was born in Tipperary, Ireland, and I really don't remember my parents at all as they died when I was young. They had both been widowed when they married each other and the children from their first unions were quite a bit older than I.

"My sister Mary, and her husband Philip Naughton, took me in, and Philip put me to work almost at once, teaching me the trade of building so I would be able to support myself. Soon we went to England as there was more building going on there than in Ireland. It was hard work, and I had to learn quickly. I was a good hand by the time I was fifteen.

"We'd not been in England very long when Philip heard about the Erie Canal and the other waterways that America was building and planning to build. He said it was the opportunity of a lifetime, and he and Mary came onto America. I sailed as soon as I could after them on a long and miserable sea voyage. As soon as I arrived in New York, I joined Philip and we headed for the Erie Canal. You know the rest of the story.

"We were fortunate enough to meet you though I barely arrived to see the work completed on the Erie later in the fall of 1825. We saw Governor Clinton pour the water from Lake Erie into the Hudson River. We should have thought of something like that for today."

"I hope these people realize the Blackstone is going to transform Worcester from a sleepy little village to a bustling city when the boat travel and transportation are up and running." Tobey continued. "We have about five hundred Irishmen who have been working on the canal. I want to keep them in the area because I intend to do a lot more construction in these parts. My next goal is to get a railroad contract, preferably the Worcester to Boston line. I have opened my store, and I intend to see that we soon have schools and a place to bury our dead. And I don't care what these Yankees think. We are going to build some Catholic Churches and get some priests to say Mass every Sunday and holy days. With finishing the canal my top priority, I haven't been able to do that, but I will."

"I'm sure that you will, Tobey," Ben said. "Here we are dedicating the Blackstone Canal, and you ought to be up on that platform being recognized."

"No more so than you, Ben," Tobey said. "Your drawings of every step of the canal were invaluable. I couldn't have done my work without your excellent engineering plan."

Almost on cue, a man approached the two men. "Excuse me, sir," he said to Wright. "Chairman Lincoln asked me to invite you to come and sit on the platform."

"That's very nice of him," Wright said. "But I would not consider coming up there without Mr. Boland here. People need to know he built this canal."

"I'll have to ask Mr. Lincoln about that," the man said. He returned shortly and informed Ben and Tobey that they both should come to the area where the dignitaries were seated. The two canal builders looked at each other knowingly as they were assigned to the second row of seats.

About that time the band struck up "Hail Columbia" and Tobey and Ben looked down the canal and saw *The Lady Carrington* coming around a bend, moving slowly toward the dock. Banners were unfurled and flying, and the sounds of shouts and clapping filled the air. Bells rang and cannons boomed.

The boat was painted a bright white with red curtains that fluttered in the slight breeze. Her decks were filled with men dressed in cutaway coats and top hats and ladies who wore colorful gowns and large hats covered with feathers.

On the deck of *The Lady Carrington,* the dignitaries waved and smiled. The four large horses in tandem that pulled the flat-bottomed boat slowed and their three drivers guided the barge to a pier where it was tied up.

One of the Worcester citizens, Pliny Merrick, moved forward to speak from the bow. The band finished playing as Merrick unfolded his note cards from his pocket. The crowd quietly waited in anticipation of the forthcoming remarks.

"I think this is going to be a long afternoon," Ben Wright whispered to Tobey.

His prediction was correct. John Davis and Levi Lincoln, two of the dignitaries seated on the stage had much to say after a local pastor was called to give an invocation. Lincoln traced the history of the canal and told how John Brown from Providence, Rhode Island presented his original petition back in 1796. Finally, he added, the job had finally been completed and on this glorious day the first barge had traveled the length of the new canal.

Lincoln described the size of *The Lady Carrington,* and noted it was named after Commissioner Carrington's wife. He said the barge was seventy and one-half feet long and seven feet wide, and had navigated sixty-two locks on the fourteen-hour trip from Providence.

Tobey noticed Isaiah Thomas, editor and printer of ***The Massachusetts Spy***, a noted newspaper in Worcester, was busy taking notes as the various speeches were given.

Finally a last announcement was made that a reception would be held at Levi Lincoln's palatial home on Elm Street. Wright was invited and accepted, but Tobey shook his head and declined. Turning to Ben he said, "I have to go see a man about buying some land. Enjoy this while you can, Ben,"

"What do you mean?" Ben asked.

"What I mean is that the Blackstone Canal is going to bring prosperity and growth to the village of Worcester right now. This canal will have a few years, maybe as many as twenty, and then the Blackstone will have served its purpose and lived its life. You can bet Boston isn't going to sit still and let Worcester become the industrial center of Massachusetts.

"Take a good look now, Ben," Tobey went on, "because in the next twenty-five years the steam engine and the railroads will make this waterway obsolete."

Ben nodded in agreement. "For a young man, you have a lot of perception. And I know you're right," he said. "Railroads are the wave of the future. I hope you and Philip Naughton learned the trade of building railroads when you were in England as well as you learned how to dig canals."

CHAPTER SEVEN

Tobey got up from the desk where he was sorting invoices and other papers. The store was up and running and time was passing so fast. It had taken Tobey a year to finalize the Blackstone Canal business, get his contracting fees, pay the crew, and stock his new store. New Year's Day of 1831 had just passed and it was time to go and get his new wife. He knew he had hesitated because of the edict issued by Dr. McCauley that the marriage must take place in the Baptist Church. His last letter from Mary Ellen indicated she was becoming impatient and tired of waiting. She made no mention of her father's present attitude. Tobey thought he should plan to travel south as soon as possible.

Tobey got up and moved to a large pile of boxes in the center of the store. He picked up one of the large boxes and moved it to another area.

"You're really strong," said Terry O'Shea, standing nearby. Terry was struggling to pick up a second similar box.

"It's from working hard building canals and other things," Tobey smiled and moved over to help Terry with the large box.

"You've been building canals a long time, haven't you?" Terry said.

"Since I was in my early teens," Tobey said. "Sometimes it seems I have been doing it all my life."

Terry looked at Tobey with admiration.

"I know I'm newly here from Ireland, and I wish I had someone to teach me all you know. I want to be wise and strong like you."

"It takes a good mentor," Tobey said. "I was lucky to have my brother-in-law, Philip Naughton, to show me the way. We went from Ireland to England when I was just a boy. He taught me the work and how to plan projects. As I grew older and stronger, he let me take part in the heavy work. In England we built not only canals, but bridges and buildings. Now that the Blackstone Canal is finished and operating, I want to build a railroad."

"But running the store, how will you have time to keep on being a contractor?" Terry asked.

Tobey smiled. "And why do you think I've brought you all the way here from Ireland, lad?"

Tobey patted Terry on the back. "Never think I'm done with building, Terry. There'll be plenty of jobs soon enough. I want to build better quarters for the workers and houses and churches, especially churches. That's something that lasts and has meaning. But as for being strong physically, that's helpful, but there is another part."

Tobey placed his hand on Terry's shoulder. "You must have the mind to want to learn and the patience to keep after a task until you master it. You did well working on the canal and you drive the horses well. Stay with me, Terry, and I'll try to show you the way just as Philip did for me."

"I would be most grateful. Where's Philip now?" Terry asked.

"He's down in Washington, D.C. finding more things to build and more worlds to conquer. I'm about to go to Washington to get a young lady there and make her my wife. Then I want to get back here and get the contract for building a railroad between

Worcester and Boston. That will be our next big project, I hope."

The conversation was interrupted by the sound of shouts and scuffling outside the front of Tobey's store.

"What's going on?" Tobey said, and moved toward the front door. He looked outside to see three large rough-looking men surrounding another man.

One of the rough fellows pushed the better dressed man, shouting, "You can't shop here." Tobey was shocked to see it was Benjamin Wright.

"It's Ben," he shouted to Terry. "Come on." And Tobey was outside in a flash and grabbed the offender by the neck of his coat.

"Take your dirty hands off this gentleman," Tobey shouted in the ear of the thug. Another one of the gang moved in toward Tobey, but he was too slow. Tobey dropped the first fellow, turned and hit the second man in the jaw, sending him sprawling. The third man came toward Tobey, who pushed the first offender into the charging man and raised his fist again.

"Get away from here," Tobey snarled. "Get off this property and stay off." He took a step toward the three who began to back away.

"We'll be back," one muttered. "We won't allow you Irishmen to take over our town."

"We're here to stay," Tobey answered. "I mean it. Be gone with you, or the next time you won't be able to walk away."

Terry had stepped between Wright and the three. As the group moved slowly away, looking back over their shoulders, Tobey turned his attention to Ben.

"Ben," he said, "I'm so sorry for this incident."

"Not your fault," Ben said. "They said I couldn't buy from your store, but I told them that where I shopped was my business and not theirs. They've been following me for about a block. I see what you mean, however, about the Irish not being welcomed. But this is too much. Worcester will never become and important industrial center with this attitude. The canal has begun some successful operation and they're acting like a bunch of ruffians."

"Come on inside, Ben," Tobey said. "They're gone for now, and we can talk. What brings you shopping at Boland's Merchandise Store today anyway?"

"I wanted to buy a new shirt," Ben said, "But more than that, I want to talk to you."

They moved to the back of the building where counters and shelves lined the rear of the store. Terry brought up two chairs, but then backed behind a counter where he continued to stand.

"Is Nathan Heard still buying the entire contents of the canal barges?" Ben asked.

"That's what I hear. I wonder what price he'll put on all that salt and grain he's ordering. Since his has been an accepted business for many years, he doesn't have the unruly reception committee that my store does. But then he's not a Catholic."

"It has to get better, Tobey," Ben said. "Merchants and citizens must cooperate. But that's not what I want to talk to you about."

"What might that be?" Tobey asked.

"I have news from Washington," Ben began. "I want to go there and learn about upcoming railroad contracts and new projects are in this area. I want you to go with me. Isn't Philip Naughton still in that area?"

"Yes, he is," Tobey replied, "And where there are contracts to be had, Philip will be in the midst of things. And I'm ready for a new construction job—and perhaps a new life. Before we leave for Washington, I want to buy some land. When all else is lost, land is the only thing that remains and matters. I'll be building a home and one day a church and school around here. For that I will need the land."

"Good thinking," Ben said. "But land costs money, and you'll need more construction jobs to raise capital for that land and those new building ventures."

"You're right. I want the Boston and Worcester Railroad contract. I will go with you to Washington. I'll have to find someone to keep the store while I'm gone, however." Tobey looked straight at Terry. "I think I have the man to do it already. Yes, count on me to go with you. When do we leave?"

"As soon as we can get travel arrangements," Ben said. "We can take the Blackstone to Providence and then switch to overland carriage. I'll let you know as soon as I can secure our passage. Now let me see about buying a new shirt."

Tobey and Terry showed Ben the men's shirts in stock, and Ben selected one to his liking and left shortly thereafter. Tobey accompanied him to the front door and checked outside to be sure the hecklers had gone. They had.

When they came back inside, Tobey looked at Terry and said, "It's you I mean to keep the store, you know."

"Do you think I'm ready to handle it?" Terry asked.

Tobey frowned. "I wouldn't be asking you to do the job if I didn't think you could handle it. The important thing is that you not only think but *know* you can do it. Desire and determination are the first two characteristics for success. You remember that, and learn everything you can every chance you get. You never know when you may need it."

Terry threw back his shoulders. "Yes, sir, I can handle this store, and I will do a fine job for you."

"That's more like it," Tobey smiled again. "Now let's finish moving these boxes."

"Can I ask you another question?" Terry said. "How'd you learn to fight? You scared those guys right off the walkway."

"Practice," Tobey said. "You don't run a canal building crew without showing them who is boss. Being tall and muscular comes from working in construction but the mental part is also important. And never show any fear. Never let your opponent know you are afraid. Be bold and assert yourself in all circumstances."

Tobey found he had to call upon all his own advice when he attempted to buy land. The owners of the property he had selected for building a church were ready to sign over the deed until the property owners asked what use he planned for the land. When Tobey told him that he would build a Catholic church on the lot, the owners quickly backed out of the deal.

Tobey relayed this information to Ben Wright.

"Let me see what I can do." Ben said.

The next day Tobey found that Ben had arranged for another buyer to obtain the land. That buyer then agreed to sell it to Tobey.

"I can't thank you enough," Tobey said to Ben when they had completed the land sale and Tobey held the deed to the property he wanted.

"Glad to be of help," Ben said, "But get your bags packed. We leave in two days for Washington."

Tobey and Terry watched Ben as he left. There had been no hecklers since his first store visit and Tobey's threat to the trouble makers.

"Terry," Tobey said. "Take a good look at Benjamin Wright. That man will go down in the history of this country as the father of civil engineering in America."

Tobey watched Ben walk away. "And, he is one of the best friends I'll ever have."

He hurried to begin his packing. The thought of seeing Mary Ellen again excited him. On the long journey ahead he would have to think about how he could obtain permission from Dr. McCauley to marry his daughter. The memory of his last conversation with the Baptist minister still disturbed Tobey. Would he have to agree to become a Baptist? Mary Ellen was well worth it, but what a price to have to pay for a wife!

CHAPTER EIGHT

Tobey was instructing Terry O'Shea in matters of keeping the store as he stacked his travel bags beside the counter.

A man entered the establishment.

"Are you Mr. Tobias Boland?" the man asked.

"I am."

"I have a letter for you here. The postal clerk told me I might be able to find you at this store since he had sent other postal pieces to you here." The man handed the letter to Tobey who recognized Philip's handwriting at once. He tore off the seal of the square folded epistle, opened it and began to read.

My dear Tobey,

I am sorry to tell you that the Reverend Doctor McCauley has died. Your Mary Ellen is not only grief stricken but in dire financial straits. It seems her father had debts that were excessive. The Baptists have already taken over the house in which she and her mother lived. We are presently allowing them to stay with us, but Mrs. McCauley has a sister in Virginia and they are planning to go and live with her any day.

If you still have plans to marry Mary Ellen, I suggest you come at once or she may be lost to you forever. Mary and I will do what we can for Mary Ellen and her mother, but you need to come quickly.

Your obedient servant and devoted brother-in-law, Philip

Tobey sighed. "Bad news, Boss?" Terry McShea asked.

"Yes and no," Tobey said. He handed Terry the letter.

"Good thing you were planning to leave today," Terry said. "And don't worry about a thing. We'll take care of everything here at the store."

Tobey rushed off to meet Ben Wright, and in a short time they were on a barge going down the Blackstone Canal. They had hoped it would be *The Lady Carrington*, but that barge was on the other end of the waterway.

Tobey updated Ben on the letter he had just received.

"I'm sorry to hear of the death of Dr. McCauley," Ben said. "He had a lot of influence in the community."

"And on his daughter as well," Tobey said. "Although he never gave his permission for us to marry, it is my understanding that now his wife and daughter are left in financial straits. My plan is for the wedding to take place as soon as possible. I can't imagine that her mother will have any objection under the circumstances."

Tobey was very sorry Mary Ellen had lost her parent, but he was greatly relieved that her father's death removed the need for his approval or for any church affiliation demands. He was even more anxious to see Mary Ellen, be married, and return to Worcester--and best of all without becoming a Baptist.

Tobey turned his attention to the Blackstone Canal and said to Ben. "These canal locks seem to be working very satisfactorily."

"Yes, the water is flowing according to the needs of the barges. How long it will take before the mill owners along this canal begin to further their complaints and lay claim to the water itself? Some are already hostile about the Blackstone. That's hard to understand because the canal is increasing their prosperity by the added sale of their mill produce and the ease of getting raw materials."

"The canal is superior to pulling loads by oxen teams," Tobey said. "But Philip wrote me earlier that they have started laying tracks for what will be the Baltimore and Ohio Railroad. That began the same year the Blackstone opened. I still strongly think that the railroads will take over the commerce along the east coast very soon."

"You are right of course. Still, for this trip, we will have to get a coach for that last thirty miles from Baltimore to Washington, The news is that President John Quincy Adams is supporting national improvement of highways, canals, and even weather stations, but he doesn't have long left in his term as president. He's also had a lot of opposition since he was chosen president by the House of Representatives even though Andrew Jackson got the popular vote. And Jackson is bound to get the presidency this time and what a contrast that will be--Adams with his short and stout body and his shrill voice, and Jackson the real frontier man.

"But we'll leave the politics to the others, Tobey, our job is to build."

"I just ordered a copy of James Fennimore Cooper's new book called *The Last of the Mohicans*." Tobey said.

"That's interesting," Ben smiled. "I have just ordered the two volumes of Webster's new dictionary.

Let's hope the new legislation being called *The Monroe Doctrine* will keep war factions away so we can read and build."

When the two travelers finally arrived in Washington, they parted company and Tobey went to the home of Philip and Mary Naughton as fast as he could.

Mary Ellen rushed into Tobey's arms as soon as he entered the house. She clung fiercely to him, and he might have been embarrassed had he not been so glad to see her.

Tobey smiled to note she was still the lovely girl he had left too very long ago, but now she had the mature look of a young woman. Yet sadness filled her face and she clung to Tobey.

"I'm so glad you are finally here, Tobey," she said. "With you, I know things will be all right. Oh, Tobey, never leave me again, please. Promise me you will never leave me again."

Tobey was overjoyed to hear those words. Mary Ellen had indeed waited for him. He was very happy, but he was not sure what to say.

"My deepest sympathy on the loss of your father," Tobey said.

Mary Ellen looked at Tobey. "Thank you," she said.

There was an awkward silence.

Finally Tobey spoke. "If your mother will give us permission, I would like for us to be married as soon as possible."

"Oh, yes, as soon as we can," Mary Ellen said. "Mother wants to leave for her sister's in Virginia as soon as possible, and I want to go with you."

"I would like our wedding to be a Catholic ceremony," Tobey said.

Mary Ellen looked into Tobey's eyes. "I have no objection to that," she said. "I only want to be your wife and to go with you and be with you wherever you are."

With Philip's help, arrangements were made, and Tobey and Mary Ellen were married in Georgetown two weeks later, on May 28, 1831, with the ceremony performed by one of the Jesuits. The only people present were the bride and groom, Mary and Philip, Mary Ellen's mother and a girl friend of Mary Ellen's.

Two days later Mary Ellen's mother boarded a stage coach to Virginia, and three days later, Mr. and Mrs. Tobias Boland left Washington for Worcester.

Tobey found he had a different approach to Shanty Town when he and his new wife got back. The shacks which were moved by work crews as the canal work progressed were now back in place. The tents which were also used as temporary living quarters were stowed until a new construction job could be started. Tobey was pleased to find that Michael Callahan had not only improved the crew quarters, but he also had built new separate quarters for Tobey and Mary Ellen, larger and better built as well as better looking.

"With you bringing back a new missus, we figured you would need a nicer place to live," Michael said. He smiled broadly.

"Michael, you could not have done anything to please me more," Tobey said.

He took a deep breath, however, as he led his bride into the rustic building. He thought of the lavish house in Washington where she had lived most of her life.

He vowed to get a better house for them as soon as possible.

Mary Ellen was not daunted by the shabby quarters. She smiled at Tobey and said, "As long as we are together, the house in which we live is not important."

As the year 1832 dawned, Mary Ellen was heavy with child. Tobey had been working to improve the health conditions in Shanty Town and he tried without success to obtain the services of a doctor for his Irish community.

Finally a midwife was found among the Irish families and when Mary Ellen's labor pains began, she was called in.

Anxious hours went by slowly. The midwife and several other women who had come to assist would come out of the room where Mary Ellen was and announce that there was no baby yet.

Just as the sun was rising, Tobey heard a keening cry from the adjoining room. His heart beat rapidly. The midwife came out crying and wringing her hands.

"Your wife has birthed a baby girl," she screamed, "But the babe was dead on entering this world. We need a priest to come and bless us all." She went running from the house.

Tobey rushed to Mary Ellen's side. "Is my wife all right?" he demanded of the two women who were still at her bedside.

"She is sleeping," one woman replied. "We won't know for awhile if she will survive." The woman left the room with the baby wrapped in a blanket. Tobey did not ask to see the child.

Tobey sat in a chair beside Mary Ellen and put his face in his hands and wept. How could this be happening to them? He and his Mary Ellen had been so happy. They had eagerly awaited the arrival of this child.

This is my fault, Tobey thought. I have been so busy digging canals and building things, I have not tended to the physical and health needs of my own family or my workers. Physical and spiritual things have been too long neglected. We have no regular Mass said, and now when we need a priest, there is none.

He laid his head on Mary Ellen's shoulder. "We will have a priest here," Tobey said to no one in particular as the women had left the room.

This personal tragedy made Tobey determined that his family and his people would have a priest and a burying spot. No longer would they have to go to Rhode Island to bury their dead. The town of Worcester still refused to open their cemeteries to the Irish. After a great deal of negotiation about the land Tobey had bought from Newton for $75, Tatnuck Cemetery was established and become the first Irish Cemetery in the area. The French were also allowed to be buried there.

Tobey was devastated that his and Mary Ellen's daughter, who had been called Elizabeth, was one of the first graves in Tatnuck Cemetery.

Tobey refused to leave Mary Ellen's side and did his best to console her. She did recover physically, but the sadness of losing her first child remained with her for months. Tobey kept his promise to get a priest. He went to Boston several times to argue for the assignment of one. Finally, in 1832 the diocese assigned Father James Fitton, who began a circuit ride one Sunday out of every four to the Worcester area. With his traveling bag of needed elements, vestments, holy oil, candles, altar wine and missal, Father Fitton could and did hold Mass in a wide assortment of places–barns, houses, and at times in the open air.

On April 6, 1834 a congregation of about one hundred people gathered in Tobey's store to assist Father Fitton in the first public Mass celebrated in a building in the area of Worcester. No longer would they have to hold their services in the open fields.

But Father Fitton's attempts to buy land for a permanent church building were not successful at first. Pushed on by Tobey, three Protestant men--William Lincoln, Francis Blake and Harvey Pierce--purchased property for the church. They paid $600 for three lots of pasture land centrally located on a wagon track that eventually was called Temple Street. By 1836, Tobey had constructed a small frame church called Christ's Church and the congregation had paid for it.

Mary Ellen always accompanied Tobey to every Mass without question. Tobey finally found a young and dedicated doctor who agreed to come to Shanty Town periodically and treat the Irish who were sick or hurt. Illness was still rampart with dysentery and tuberculosis taking the lives of many of the Irish living in Shanty Town. Immigrant Irish were arriving with an illness called 'ship fever' and they never recovered their health. Far too many women were dying with the dreaded "child birth fever." Tobey secured clean water for the community and attempted sewage control though neither was easy nor entirely successful. Tobey knew that unless he could improve the living conditions of Shanty Town, the population of Tatnuck Cemetery would increase rapidly.

As he could, Tobey continued to purchase more property. He was able to buy five acres near Green Street where he began to build his much longed for new house. In 1832 another child was born to the couple, their first son. He was named John after Tobey's father. Tobey had kept to himself his great concern for Mary Ellen's health, but she had no problems with this birth. A second son soon followed and he was named Francis, Tobey's middle name, but he was always called Frank. With a growing family, Tobey also sought more construction work, expanded his business and strengthened his holdings in the Worcester area.

Tobey had always believed the future of commerce for the country lay with railroads. In 1835, after many trips and much argument, he was successful in obtaining the contract to build a railroad from Boston to Worcester. Tobey's prophecy about the future of the United States being in railroads was about to be fulfilled.

CHAPTER NINE

Tobey's work on the Blackstone Canal had given him a reputation for reliable construction and confirmed his ability to recruit and control workers. Many of the Irish crews had remained in Shanty Town and were available to pick up their traveling shacks and begin construction on short notice on another job. The latest was the Boston and Worcester Railroad.

The legislature had incorporated the Boston and Worcester Railroad in 1831, for it had not escaped the notice of Boston that with the opening of the Blackstone Canal, Worcester merchants were increasing their supplies through Providence rather than Boston. They could not allow this to happen. And so the push to complete the Boston and Worcester Railroad became important, and because of his sterling reputation as a builder and contractor, Tobey was awarded the contract.

Work commenced at once and by 1833 Tobey and his Irish workers had brought the railway halfway along its forty-four mile stretch between the two towns. The course was gradually rising to Worcester on the eastern border where the rail bed had to take a sharp detour to the south to get around Lake Quinsigamond. West of the lake, the roadbed turned north between the lake and the eastern flank of Sagatabscot Hill. Here there was only a narrow separation between the hill and the shore of the lake and cuts had to be made through solid granite.

"We've never hit such hard digging," Michael Callahan said to Tobey as they stood overlooking the lay of the land beneath them. "We can't get through here with only picks and shovels," Michael continued. "We will have to use black blasting powder."

"You're right, of course," Tobey said. "I wish we didn't have to do that because the powder is so very dangerous. I'm afraid using it will result in some bad and even fatal accidents."

"We've no choice," Michael said. "And we'll have another especially deep cut when the road turns west again to resume a direct course into the village of Worcester."

"You're right again. The track being laid from town out to Sagatabscot is moving well," Tobey said, "But to satisfy those owners who want the railroad open early in 1835, we are going to have to work into winter weather, and we've already had an early first freeze in this fall of the year 1834. But in order to complete the work satisfactorily and on schedule, we will have to go to the black powder."

Tobey's prediction was correct. Disaster struck early in the year 1835 when two workers were killed in a black powder explosion. Another worker was crushed to death in a rock slide and three more perished in another rock slide. Work in the frigid temperatures of February, 1835 was deadly and still another Irish worker fell to his death from icy rocks. A March snowstorm brought another accidental powder blast, and on that same day, another faulty explosion sent rocks down on a shanty Irish camp and injured women and children living in the flimsy structures.

When the last of these events occurred, the workers put down their tools and refused to continue working. Supervisors dismissed them from the camps, but then they refused to leave. Tobey, along with contractor William Lomasney, was called by the railroad company officials to come at once to the scene.

Tobey brought with him the Reverend James Fitton, pastor of the Irish immigrants in the Worcester area. Mediation began and numerous conferences were held. The meetings of these authorities resulted in many changes and conditions were improved. Tobey secured higher pay for the workers. The women and children were moved to the safer neighborhood of the Irish settlement at Pine Meadow on the eastern edge of town.

Work on the railroad resumed and was finally completed. On July 6, 1835 the Boston and Worcester railroad opened with a grand celebration in Worcester. Tobey brought Mary Ellen who was aglow with the attention and honors bestowed on Tobey. He was thanked for his contribution and even asked to speak a few words.

The opening of the new railroad gave Worcester a connection to Boston in the first of a series of movements that improved access to raw materials and markets and launched the village into a major inland manufacturing center. Tobey's foresight in predicting the railroad's impact gained new respect for his opinions. His engineering abilities made him a rich man and brought him continued contracts and an even higher opinion of his abilities as a builder. He became known as the fellow who could do a good job and have it ready on time.

As soon as the Boston and Worcester Railroad was completed, and with funds now in his possession, Tobey set out to build what he had dreamed of for so long--a church for the Irish community. Father Fitton was now permanently assigned to Worcester and he and Tobey worked together on the plans for this sanctuary and set about to erect the first church building.

Tobey, who had always been interested and ambitious for more education, also committed to provide Father Fitton with two wooden academy buildings which were in the future to serve as St. James Academy. He set about to procure land arrangements so this needed educational project could begin to grow.

Things were going so well that Mary Ellen was surprised when Tobey came in one night in a mood of depression.

"What is it?" she asked.

"They called me a foreigner," Tobey told her. "I've been in this country a dozen years and they called me a foreigner."

"Who called you that?" Mary Ellen asked.

"Some of my business associates, bankers. Even Benjamin Wright said that I needed to apply for United States citizenship. As long as I'm considered an Irishman, there will be prejudice against me. It could keep my business from continued growth and have a bearing on my reputation as a contractor."

Mary Ellen smiled. "Well, then, I think you should apply for citizenship. You might even get a warmer welcome in Worcester if you were a real United States citizen."

After thinking about this for several days, Tobey decided he was never going to return to Ireland to live. Even the memory of his seasickness made him shudder. This country was his home and here he would live and die, so he decided he should become a full citizen.

And so on April 21, 1837 Tobey appeared before the magistrate in the County of Worcester and became a naturalized citizen of the United States of America.

Mary Ellen with her usual good humor said, "I'm certainly glad I'm no longer married to a foreigner." That remark caused even Tobey to laugh. He was well aware that his Baptist-reared bride had put up with so many hardships without complaining, and for that he was grateful.

The Bolands moved to their now completed new house on Green Street and Tobey's work continued to prosper. The boys were growing fast and Mary Ellen was concerned about their education. The Irish were still not accepted in the Worcester schools, so Mary Ellen suggested she start a school in the Boland home and teach her own children as well as those of some of the Irish neighbors until they were old enough to attend Father Fitton's St. James Academy. Tobey agreed that this was a splendid idea. He promptly hired two Irish girls to move in as domestics and help with the household duties and attend to the children which freed Mary Ellen to do some of the teaching.

Father Fitton still had dreams of his proposed academy, but he was in favor of Mary Ellen's idea and offered his cooperation. Since Tobey was gone from home so much on contracting jobs, he left the running of the house and the raising of the children to Mary Ellen and the two Irish domestics. The classes began and were successful beyond anticipation.

In keeping with his promise to the priest, Tobey built a school for Father Fitton which was called St. James Academy. It was located at Green and Temple Street. Mary Ellen moved some of her classes and teaching there as they were outgrowing the house. Father Fitton was pleased with these developments but he did not lose sight of his idea to have a Catholic boarding school for boys. He dreamed of obtaining a larger property out from town with room to expand. It disturbed the good father that the Baptists had in 1834 opened the Worcester Country Manuel Labor High School. He hoped that the bishop, the Right Reverend Benedick Fenwick, who was a Jesuit, would join him in this quest for Jesuit education in New England.

On January 22, 1836, with the help of Tobey, Father Fitton bought a tract of land for $2000 cash in the southwestern part of the town on the northerly side of Bogachoag Hill. This was part of the farm of Henry Patch who had recently died. The land had a house and a barn on it. With the largest donation from Tobey Boland, Father Fitton solicited other funds and he and Tobey moved St. James Academy to Pakachoag Hill. Tobey not only pledged the necessary funds, but he sent his Irish crews to construct two wooden buildings on the property. One was a two story structure seventy feet long which was to contain classrooms. The other was a modest cottage which would serve as the residence for priests. Father Fitton placed the farm under the management of his younger brother, Abraham, and notified Bishop Fenwick in Boston to send his representative to survey the program.

St. James Academy had a new home indeed, but neither Father Fitton nor Tobey could imagine the success that would come from this humble beginning.

Tobey was pleased that progress was being made in so many undertakings, but in spite of his efforts to improve the health and living conditions for the Irish, far too many still died from a number of sicknesses and diseases.

Tobey was not to be spared. Early in 1840, Mary Ellen gave birth to a baby boy named Robert. The baby survived only a little while, and after several terrible days of suffering, Tobey's beloved Mary Ellen succumbed to the dreaded "child birth fever." Tobey frantically summoned doctors, midwives, and Father Fitton to come to her bedside. They prayed and they waited, but there was nothing they could do to save Mary Ellen. On the last day of her life, she looked at Tobey who had not left her bedside for hours, and smiled. "Take care of the children," she said, and slipped from this life.

Tobey was devastated and could not be consoled. He was too distraught to make arrangements to bury his beloved wife. Terry McShea, who had become an adopted son to Tobey and Mary Ellen, and Father Fitton made the arrangements for a Requiem Mass, and Mary Ellen was laid to rest in Tatnuck Cemetery, next to the grave of her first baby, Elizabeth, and baby Robert.

For weeks Tobey was unable to work. He refused to go out of the house. Michael Callahan and Terry McShea came to consult with him on building and contracting matters, but Tobey only told them to do what they thought was best. He sat in a rocking chair in the parlor by the fireplace for hours in silent meditation.

When he closed his eyes, he could see Mary Ellen in the other rocking chair with the two boys snuggled in her lap as she read to them. What would he do now that his children had no mother? Tobey tried to console John and Frank, but they did not understand where their mother was or why she was not coming back.

With the domestics, the household was surviving even as Tobey sank into further depression. He seldom came to the table for a meal; in fact he seldom ate at all. Sitting by the fireside, he would drink a cup of tea or sip some Irish whiskey.

Sitting in his chair, he dwelt on his memories with Mary Ellen. They were all he had left, he thought, because his dreams of a future with her by his side would never be. His sister's words, spoken long ago, came again to his mind: *To be Irish is to know that in the end, the world will break your heart.*

Father Fitton finally lured Tobey out of the house to go to Boston with him on a mission to secure more land for the academy he had in mind to enlarge. He needed Tobey to act as agent for the diocese in order to purchase the needed property, and he also wanted the bishop to meet and know Tobey. At his own expense, Toby had erected the wooden two story academy building being used as the school, and he had also built a small structure where Father Fitton resided.

"Miss Mary Ellen was so in favor of education," Father Fitton said to Tobey. "You know she would want you to be a part of continuing to build better facilities for the children here. Come with me to Boston. Your knowledge and your backing will be needed for this project."

And so in June of 1840 Tobey and Father Fitton set out for Boston to meet with Bishop Benedict Joseph Fenwick, S.J., the second bishop of the diocese that covered almost the entire New England region. The bishop was now caught up in the idea of founding an educational institution in the area, and since he himself was a Jesuit, he wanted that order to head the institution.

In Boston, Toby not only met the bishop; he also met Father John Bernard Fitzpatrick who had recently been ordained on June 13. Before the chancery meeting at to discuss the property to be purchased, Tobey was introduced to Father Fitzpatrick's sister, Eleanor Fitzpatrick.

He was surprised that a woman was involved in such a meeting, but Father Fitton told him that the new priest and his sister were very close. She was a woman of note in literary circles, educated in Boston, and the first woman to teach Latin and Greek in the public schools of New England, a most unusual position for a woman. She was also an author and a weekly contributor in the magazines printed in Boston and New York using the nom de plume "Alethe." She was tall and slender, a very attractive woman with dark hair and piercing brown eyes. Her speech was articulate, and she spoke with elegance and knowledge about educational needs, securing property and building schools.

Tobey was impressed, and for the first time since Mary Ellen's death, he was aware of the presence of a woman.

CHAPTER TEN

When Tobey went to answer the doorbell early one morning, he found Terry O'Shea standing there.

"God bless all in this house," Terry said, "I'm here with your carriage."

"Oh, yes," Tobey answered. "Today is the day we go to Pakachoag Hill and meet with the bishop about St. James Academy. Come on in while I get my things ready to go."

Now able to afford his own transportation, Tobey had bought the coach and horses. With the travel requirements of his contracting business, it was much more practical to be able to come and go as necessary. Terry had been his driver arriving from Ireland just before the opening of the Blackstone Canal; he had become invaluable to Tobey as a working assistant, a friend, and an adopted son.

Soon the two boarded the coach and, as they drove out toward Pakachoag Hill, Terry pointed out to Tobey that the temperature was dropping and a stiff breeze was blowing the carriage with some force.

"We've got a northeastern storm coming in," Terry said. "There'll be bad weather, maybe as soon as tonight."

"Then it is good we have our meeting early today," Tobey said and surveyed the clouds that were racing across the sky.

The bishop himself did not come, but instead he sent the new priest, Father John Fitzpatrick, and once more, to Tobey's surprise, Eleanor was with her brother.

"While Father Fitton and I survey the land and buildings, Eleanor will go to the classrooms and inquire about the curriculum and teaching methods," Father John explained. "Will you be good enough, Mr. Boland, to accompany my sister Eleanor and answer any questions she may have regarding the need for adding additional space?"

Tobey knew he had no choice but to abide by the wishes of the priest, but he actually did not mind; and he and Eleanor proceeded to the two-story building he had recently erected.

"I understand you provided the funds and constructed this building," Eleanor said.

Tobey looked at her, uncertain how to answer her statement.

"I believe education to be of great importance for success in life," Tobey said.

"It was a noble thing to do, nonetheless," Eleanor said.

They walked on quietly and entered the classroom building.

"We'll just observe the classes," Eleanor said. "And when the boys are dismissed, we can find out more detail if need be. I have read with interest Father Fitton's educational objectives, stating that the course of instruction would comprise all the branches of a sound, correct and practical English education such as will qualify youth for usefulness in the various avocations of life."

"That is his aim," Tobey said. "He also stresses that they be well grounded in the essential rudiments of spelling, reading, and grammar. My wife–"Tobey paused as his throat tightened.

Eleanor looked at him with compassion. "I am so sorry to learn of the death of your wife," Eleanor said quietly. "My brother informed me of your recent sorrow. It is my understanding that she was a great promoter of education. Being a single person, I cannot possibly conceive of your grief."

Tobey took a deep breath. "Thank you. Yes, I was about to say Mary Ellen advocated that students move on to writing, arithmetic and book keeping, and geography illustrated by the use of maps and globes, and ancient and modern history."

"That is a commendable course of study with which I whole-heartedly agree," Eleanor said. "I notice many youthful and husky Irish laborers here in these classes. Is that also your doing?"

"I encourage it. They are idle from construction projects during the slack winter season and eager to seize any educational opportunity here in the land of promise. Also, their brawn is transforming Pakachoag Hill into a monument to their physical training program. They have earned the title of Mound Builders for their efforts."

Tobey and Eleanor listened to lectures and lessons from the back of the room and then moved on to other classrooms and the small library. Eleanor made notes in a small black notebook.

About noon, they were summoned to join the two priests in the dining hall where lunch was served to them by some of the students. The sun had gone behind the increasing gray clouds which were gathering rapidly.

"We decided our tour is over for today," Father Fitton said. "It will begin to rain any minute."

As the group prepared to return to Worcester and on to Boston, the storm predicted by Terry O'Shea was bearing down fiercely on the area. They hurried to board their respective coaches.

Tobey approached Father Fitzpatrick. "It is not safe for you to travel back to Boston in this weather. May I offer you the hospitality of my home for the night?"

Father John looked at his sister, then back to Tobey. "I think that is a splendid idea, don't you, Eleanor? Mr. Boland, we will be honored to accept your offer for our overnight at your house."

"Then have your driver follow my carriage. Once we arrive, Terry will see to your horse and driver being taken care of for the night as well."

Tobey presided over the evening meal. He had not done so for several months, and he felt ill at ease. The storm continued to increase. The wind roared against the outside of the house and rain beat upon the windows in great gusts. A chill had descended over the house, and after the meal, Tobey had the Irish domestic, Bridget, light the fire in the parlor. He invited his guests to join him there.

Father John requested that he be excused to his bedroom for his evening breviary, but Eleanor came along to the parlor with Tobey.

As they sat awkwardly in the two rocking chairs without conversation, Tobey's sons John and Frank came into the room.

"Papa, can you read to us?" they asked quietly.

"Not tonight, lads. You can see we have a visitor. Get Bridget to read to you."

"But Papa," John said, "She doesn't know all the words."

Tobey looked at Eleanor and felt the color rising in his face. "I'm afraid Bridget is still learning to read."

Eleanor leaned back in the rocking chair. "Do you have the book with you?"

"Yes, here it is." John pushed the book forward.

"Then come and sit beside me and I will read to you," Eleanor said, and beckoned the boys to her chair.

Tobey watched with a catch in his throat as Eleanor Fitzpatrick took his two sons, one on each side of her, and opened the book and began to read.

Outside the storm continued to rage, but it was not as fierce as the one in Tobey Boland's mind.

No one could ever take his Mary Ellen's place, but could this lovely and learned woman become a mother to his children? They needed a mother badly. He remembered Mary Ellen's last words to him, "Take care of the children." How could he, a single man, take care of the children and continue his work in a career that required his being away so much? He also knew that he needed female companionship. It is not good for a man to be alone, he thought. Would this lady even consider his proposal? Would it be fair to Eleanor to ask so soon after Mary Ellen had died? What would her brother the priest think?

While deep in these thoughts, Tobey felt a small tug at his sleeve. "Good night, Papa," said his son John. "We thanked the nice lady for reading to us."

The boys left the room and Tobey faced Eleanor. "I thank you, too, nice lady," he said. "That was a kind gesture for you to read to my sons."

"It was my pleasure," Eleanor said, and she turned and left the room as Tobey continued to stare into the fire. That he even thought of another marriage had startled him, and now it worried him.

"What shall I do, Mary Ellen?" he whispered and closed his eyes. "Take care of the children."

Tobey heard a slight noise behind him and turned to see his young son John standing in the doorway clad in his sleeping gown.

"What is it John?" Tobey asked.

"Papa, I'm afraid," John sniffed.

"Ah now, lad, there's nothing to be afraid of. The storm has about passed. You must go and get in your bed and go to sleep."

John rushed forward and threw his arms around his father's leg. "I'm afraid because Mama has gone away and she isn't coming back, is she?"

Tobey felt a great heaviness in his chest and took a deep breath. How can you explain grief to a lad of his age? Tobey thought. How do you explain it to anyone? Finally Tobey spoke.

"No, son, your Mama has gone to heaven and she'll not be coming back, but we'll see her again one day."

"But when?" insisted John. "When will she come back and read to us again?"

Tobey could not answer for the lump in his throat and the stinging in his eyes. Finally he said, "Not for a very long time. You'll have to get Bridget to read to you or learn to read for yourself."

"Bridget doesn't know how to read," John said his voice trembling. "Could the nice lady stay and read to us again?" The boy looked at his father with tears spilling from his eyes.

"Perhaps we should ask her," Tobey said. "We'll have to ask her. Come now, I'll walk with you up to your bed."

CHAPTER ELEVEN

By the time his next trip to Boston came about, Tobey had made up his mind to talk to the Rev. John Fitzpatrick about marriage to his sister. Tobey had been informed by Father Fitton that the parents of John and Eleanor were deceased and thus Tobey concluded that if he were to ask for the hand of Miss Eleanor, he would have to get permission from her brother.

The purpose of the trip was further discussion of Father Fitton's Saint James Seminary which had been established in 1837 and was surviving if not actually thriving. Father Fitton was working very diligently for St. James to become a Jesuit seminary. His ambition was naturally favored by Bishop Benedict Fenwick who was himself a Jesuit. Tobey supported this venture as he was aware of the recent construction of several Protestant schools in the area. If the children of the Irish pioneers and settlers were ever to have a Catholic education near their homes in New England, this would be a big step in that direction.

The men spent all the next day discussing the procedure they would have to put in place to have the bishop and the Jesuits accept Father Fitton's proposal. Tobey sat quietly most of the meeting only answering questions pertaining to construction. He assured the priests that there was enough land and that it would be suitable for more building and expansion when that became necessary. He had already offered his services as a contractor and had shown his dedication to the school by his loans of both money and labor.

The meeting broke up at noon and the bishop invited Father Fitzpatrick, Tobey, and Father Fitton to join him for lunch. As the meal was completed, the bishop retired to his quarters and Tobey turned to Father Fitzpatrick and said, "Father, I wonder if I might speak with you about a personal matter?"

"Certainly," said the priest.

Father Fitton said, "Then I will leave you two to privacy and go and see to our carriage being ready for our return journey. Thank you for your help in planning the future of St. James," he said.

Tobey suddenly felt uncomfortable and unable to put his request into words.

Finally Father John spoke. "What is it you wished to speak to me about?"

"Your sister," Tobey blurted. "What I mean is I would like to talk to you about your sister."

"And what about my sister?"

Tobey cleared his throat. "You are aware that my wife died only about a year ago."

Father John nodded. "My condolences. May her soul rest in peace."

Tobey continued. "Thank you." He paused. "While I still grieve for Mary Ellen, a man cannot live alone, especially when his children are in great need of a mother. I observe that your sister is not only a very intelligent woman, but a person of compassion and kindness. We had a chance to talk during your visit to the school, and when you stayed overnight at my house at that time, she read to my two boys. She seemed to have a way with children." He paused and looked at the priest.

"And…?" Father John smiled.

"Well, sir," Tobey said, "I come to ask your permission to ask for her hand in marriage."

Father John broke into a big smile. "I had an idea that was what you were going to say," he said. "It is true that Eleanor and I are very close, especially since the death of our parents, but Mr. Boland, I must tell you that if you want to marry my sister, Eleanor, you must ask her yourself. She is not only intelligent, but also quite independent, and she has a strong mind of her own."

Tobey felt a sense of some relief. "When do you think I might possibly be able to see her and ask her?"

"I can't answer that," Father John said, "You see at the present time she is on an extended visit to the Ursuline Convent in Montreal. And you should know that she is seriously considering joining the order."

Tobey was struck dumb. Of all the answers he might have expected from the priest, this was one he had never considered.

"When will she be back?" Tobey finally asked.

"I can't answer that either," Father John said, "But I can answer your first question. Should she decide that being a nun is not her vocation, I would certainly recommend you as a husband. I have been impressed with your work, your philosophy, your dedication to the Church, which, by the way, has not escaped the notice of my sister. Should she seek my counsel, I will advise her that I think you would make a fine husband."

"Thank you," Tobey said, and stood to leave. "Thank you, and pray for me and for us that we will be guided in the right direction."

On the ride back to Worcester, Tobey was very quiet although Father Fitton chatted continually about the hope of getting the Jesuits to take over St. James. "Nothing is ever impossible," he said.

Tobey sighed. "Nothing is ever impossible," he repeated. "I hope you are right."

CHAPTER TWELVE

Tobey made two more trips to Boston. Stopping by the Bishop's offices, he found by questioning Father John that Eleanor had not returned from the convent in Montreal. The priest could not tell Tobey any more about whether or not his sister would remain in Canada and go into the convent. Tobey tried to tell himself that it might not be God's will for him to marry this woman, but he was not yet ready to believe she would never be his wife. He sadly returned to Worcester and fell into the depression that had been much of his life since Mary Ellen died.

He did resolve to see that Bridget, the Irish domestic, be allowed some time off to attend school and learn to read. He could read to the boys himself in the evening, but he was away so much that that was no solution. They were falling behind in their education, and a woman was needed in the house for many reasons.

When Tobey was alone, which was a great deal of the time by his own choice, he talked aloud to Mary Ellen about what he could do to take care of the children. She did not answer.

Tobey had recently been named the Bishop's Agent to handle matters of real estate and construction. Things moved toward Boston again, however, when Father Fitton arrived at Tobey's house early one morning and asked if Tobey could take him to Boston. The priest explained that several Jesuits from Georgetown were to be in town to meet with Bishop Fenwick and Father Fitton wanted to present his case in person for having St. James become a

Jesuit boarding school and explain some of the physical plans for future expansion.

Tobey dreaded the trip, for it saddened him to be in Boston and not be able to see Eleanor. He hoped for an answer for his now intense desire to make her his wife. Father Fitton had no transportation of his own, and Tobey was obliged as the Bishop's Agent to be present at the meeting. Tobey ordered his carriage and had Terry O'Shea drive them the forty-some miles to the Bishop's office in Boston.

The ride was not filled with much conversation. Terry and the priest assumed that Tobey was still bereaved and left him to his thoughts. But what Tobey was thinking was that it was useless for him to go to Boston again to seek a woman who had obviously decided to join a convent in Canada.

The travelers were greeted at the door of the rectory by Father John Fitzpatrick who had now been assigned to Bishop Benedict Fenwick as a secretary-assistant. As Father John guided them into the bishop's chambers, he whispered to Tobey, "She's back. Eleanor has returned to Boston."

Tobey felt a jolt of surprise and a burst of adrenalin at such news and wondered if he had heard correctly. He turned to ask Father John for more information, but there was no chance for conversation as the group was ushered into the office of the bishop who awaited them with four Jesuits from Georgetown.

A long argument began about the merits of establishing a Jesuit school and the cost and other considerations. Some of those present argued for a day school in Boston, but the bishop had become convinced the boarding school in Worcester was the most advantageous, and he pushed his fellow Jesuits to reach that decision.

Tobey was restless and found he could not concentrate on the discussion. His thoughts flew from one thing to another. If Eleanor was back, would she see him? Why had she come back? Did it mean she was not going into the convent? If he could only get out of here and talk to her.

The discussion went into theological matters that would not have interested Tobey on any day let alone today. Eleanor was back, she was somewhere in the city and he wanted very much to see her. Had she decided to go into the convent and just returned for some final settlements? Or had she decided she did not want to become a nun? He had to know.

The meeting had covered all the real estate and construction details, and as the discussion continued with more theology and the establishing of a seminary, Tobey asked to be excused with the comment that he would go and see to the where about of Terry O'Shea and the horses and their carriage. He intended to direct Terry to secure rooms for them at the local inn over night for he did not mean to leave the city until he had seen and talked to Eleanor.

He hurried down the halls looking for Father John, and to his great relief, found the priest sitting at a desk writing.

"Where is she?" Tobey burst out and then paused, realizing how loud and rude his question had been.

"Calm down, my lad," John said. "She is back in town and she is coming here to the rectory in a short while to bring me some papers from Canada. If you stay around, you can probably see her. I have not told her of the conversation you and I had some time back. I would remind you again that Eleanor is a woman of strong opinion and spirit with quite a mind of her own."

"And indeed," Tobey smiled, "That is one of the reasons why I find her such a fine candidate to be my wife."

But by mid afternoon, Eleanor had not appeared and Tobey was glad he had decided he was not leaving until he had talked to Eleanor. He announced to his fellow travelers that they would remain the night in Boston. Father Fitton would be housed at the rectory, and Terry had secured their rooms at the inn.

Finally about four o'clock, Eleanor came into Father John's office. She was dressed in a fine gown of gray wool and wore a hat of matching color. She nodded to her brother and handed him a leather pouch, and then turned to Tobey who was thinking that she looked lovelier than he had remembered. Her dark eyes sparkled and she looked straight at Tobey and smiled. She extended her hand which Tobey took and held longer than manners required.

"I hadn't expected to see you, Mr. Boland." Eleanor said.

"Nor I you," Tobey stammered. "I thought you might never come back from Montreal."

Eleanor looked strangely at Tobey, then to her brother John, and then she spoke. "I went to Montreal to try and find the answer to something that has concerned me for some time."

"I see," Tobey said with some caution.

Father John rose and came around his desk and gave his sister Eleanor an embrace.

"It is good to see you again, dear sister, and have you back in Boston," John said. "I will go and tell the housekeeper that you," and he turned to Tobey, "and your driver and Father Fitton will be staying for dinner with the bishop and Eleanor and myself. You and Eleanor can catch up on recent events until dinner is served." Father John walked out of the office.

Eleanor sat down in one of the chairs in front of the desk and motioned Tobey to take the other.

"And how are things in Worcester?" Eleanor said.

"We are still doing a lot of building," Tobey said. He did not want to engage in small talk, but was anxious to go straight to the things he had thought so many times that he would say to her.

"I have another railroad contract. But tell me, will you be going back to Montreal?"

"Why do you ask that?" Eleanor looked at Tobey and raised one eyebrow.

"Well," Tobey was at a loss for words. "Father John told me you might be contemplating going into the convent in Montreal, and I wondered if you had come to any such decision."

Eleanor stared at Tobey for a long minute. He imagined he saw a tiny glimmer of a smile. "Why would such a decision for me be of any interest to you, Mr. Boland?"

Tobey cleared his throat. Ask her now, he thought, or you may never again have the chance. "Ma'am, I am concerned to know if you have made this decision, because if you are not going into the convent, I would like to ask you to become my wife."

Eleanor leaned back in her chair and then she did smile. "Thank you, Mr. Boland; that is the nicest compliment anyone has ever paid to me."

"I need your answer," Tobey felt his pulse racing and realized he was pushing things too fast. He tried to calm his breathing.

"I have already asked permission from your brother. He told me I should ask you."

Eleanor looked down and clasped her hands together. "I am afraid there is no simple answer," she said, and Tobey's heart sank.

Eleanor looked up again, straight into Tobey's eyes. "I have not committed to any vows at this point," Eleanor said. "I still have doubts as to whether entering a convent is my calling in this life. I came back to Boston to think and pray some more about it."

Tobey let out his breath in a long sigh. There was still a chance, he thought.

"You see," Eleanor continued," My brother and I are very close, made more so by the death of our parents and the fact that now there are only the two of us. Had I been born a male, I would have entered the priesthood as he did. Being born a woman eliminates any chance of that. But I have spent a large part of my life pondering a religious vocation. I received my early education in St. Benedict Convent–the one that was burned here in 1834."

"I remember hearing of that when we were working on the railroad between here and Worcester," Tobey said. "That was a terrible thing. You must have been in great danger. How did you escape?"

"God spared me, and I have often wondered why. I might have been killed on that particular night, but I had gone home. My parents were still alive, both in poor health and my mother was sinking fast. I went to take care of her at the time of the disaster, and thus I was not in the convent when that awful riot took place during and after the fire."

"What became of the woman who was the head nun at that time?" Tobey asked. "There are a lot of strange stories about how the convent was run and what has become of her now."

"I knew Sister St. George well," Eleanor said. "There has been much controversy about her, but I found her to be an understanding woman. I met and spoke with her a number of times while I was in Montreal. It was she who encouraged me to come there and consider coming into the Ursuline order. Mary Anne Moffatt, which is her birth name, is a very intelligent woman. In fact, she was too smart for our society which likes to keep women ignorant and quiet."

Tobey listened without comment. "You know my circumstances," he said. "I loved my wife dearly but she died. You have met my children; you have visited in my home. You are aware that I have been successful as a contractor, and that I can provide well for you and my children and any children you and I might have together."

"I will be totally honest with you," Eleanor said. "I have never really thought of marriage."

"Will you think of it now?" Tobey asked. His voice was soft and almost pleading.

At that moment Father John came back into his office. He looked from Eleanor to Tobey and turned back toward the door. "It appears to me you may not have finished your conversation," he said. "I will find Father Fitton and Terry and tell them they are invited to dinner. You can continue your discussion."

But neither Eleanor nor Tobey said anything after Father John had left the room.

Finally Tobey asked, "Will you think about marriage to me?"

"I am already thinking of it," Eleanor said. "But I want to be totally honest with you about my thoughts and dreams before making such a life commitment."

"I have always thought that women are born into this world at a great disadvantage," Eleanor said. "I resent the fact that my gender has kept me from being a priest and serving God in that manner. I do not question God's intentions for my life. It is just at this time, I am not sure what those intentions are. I have become an educated woman–not an easy task, and I want to use the knowledge I possess in beneficial ways and to the glory of God. It may not have occurred to you that the only way a woman can get an education is through the church convents, and then they are allowed no other means of service other than convent life. And for some reason, I hesitate to make that commitment right now. You know the commitment is for chastity, obedience, and poverty?"

Tobey nodded. "And which of those vows would be most difficult for you?"

Eleanor paused. Finally she said, "I think the vow of obedience. Just as being a wife involves a lot of responsibility and commitment as well. A wife must obey her husband, regardless of her own opinions. She can own no property, she cannot vote. She is basically a slave. That kind of life does not appeal to me."

Eleanor looked away and stared at a painting of the Virgin Mary hanging on a wall.

"I would consider you a life partner, mother of my children, but certainly not a slave," Tobey said quickly.

"I think you truly mean that, and I know that you are a staunch supporter of education," Eleanor went on. "I am thankful to have been blessed with far more education than most women of our day. After all, I am the first woman ever allowed to teach Latin and Greek in Boston schools."

"I would encourage you to continue to teach–and learn," Tobey said.

"You also have to know that should we be blessed with children of our own, and should they show any inclination of wanting a religious vocation, you must promise not stand in their way."

"That seems to be a concern we will not face for some time to come," Tobey said, "But if and when it should come to that, I give you my word I would have no objection to having my sons become priests or my daughters become nuns, but I would want that to be their decision and not ours."

"You make a reasonable point." Eleanor said. "I also like living in Boston."

"I have a fine home in Worcester," Tobey said, "But as a contractor, I travel a great deal so there is no reason why a house in Boston could not be arranged."

"Will you love me, Mr. Boland?"

Her direct question jolted Tobey into deep silence. How could he honestly answer Eleanor? He knew he had loved Mary Ellen, and he still did so and always would, but Mary Ellen was dead, and he was not. He had the rest of his life to live, and he did not wish to live it alone. Eleanor was in his estimation an unusual and marvelous woman, and he would not lie to her.

Finally Tobey spoke. “I do not know if I can say what love is at this point, so I cannot answer that question. I can promise you I would show you the greatest of affection and be a good husband and make you my true partner in life. In time I think that could grow into a lifelong love.”

“Well spoken, Mr. Boland,” Eleanor smiled and stood up. “You must give me some time to think about this.”

Father John came in to announce that dinner was served. The dinner guests were jovial and continued the conversation regarding the establishment of the Jesuit school in Worcester. Tobey found he could not take his eyes away from the woman seated across the table from him.

Could she and would she become Eleanor Fitzpatrick Boland?

CHAPTER THIRTEEN

Tobey returned to Worcester resigned to the fact that whatever Eleanor decided would be the will of God and the Lord's plan for his life. There was nothing else he could do but wait–and see to his business which he had neglected too long.

He called a meeting of Michael Callahan and Terry O'Shea to review the current status of the construction jobs they were either working on or bidding on.

Both these men had noted a recent change in Tobey's usual melancholy disposition but said nothing of it. Terry had told Michael earlier that he suspected their boss was courting Father John's sister, but that was none of their concern, so they tactfully refrained from any mention of it.

"We're half into the year 1841, "Tobey said, "The economic panic of 1837 is over. The day of canal building is over, too, in my opinion. From now on, we must concentrate on erecting buildings and railroads. The Boston and Albany, the Worcester and Nashua and the Worcester and Harlem River contracts are our next big concern. What is our present labor situation?"

Michael Callahan spoke up. "Should we get all three of those jobs, and I think we will, we are going to need more workmen. We are still recruiting at the incoming ships in New York and Boston and hiring there. I regret to tell you that some of our Irish workers are not proving as effective as they have been on past jobs. Some are lazy and complain more than they work. They are asking for more money and fewer working hours."

"We've considered hiring Canadians before," Tobey said.

"It may come to that," Michael said, "But I personally would rather not see it. A conflict will surely arise between the two groups and will probably prove to be more of a problem than the shortage of good workers."

"Then we'll wait and see how things develop," Tobey said.

And things did develop in Tobey's life, but not in the area of his construction business. Shortly after his return from the last Boston trip, Tobey received a letter from Father John. It was short and to the point.

Come at once before she changes her mind.

Tobey had Terry ready the carriage, and they left for Boston before the setting of the sun. They arrived after dark and the rectory was closed for the night. They took rooms at the nearby inn. Bright and early the next morning, Tobey slipped into the Cathedral for the first Mass which was being said by Father John.

A lone woman sat in the front pew. Tobey recognized Eleanor and quickly said a prayer that he would today get the answer to his proposal, but he never imagined what the day would bring forth.

After the Mass Tobey hurried to the office of Father John and found the priest and his sister sitting there.

The two rose and said, "Good morning" as Tobey entered. The three of them sat down and silence prevailed. Finally Eleanor spoke. "Mr. Boland, I have decided to accept your proposal of marriage under the terms we discussed recently."

Tobey stood and smiled. "Your decision makes me very happy," he said. "When can we plan for the ceremony to take place?"

Eleanor looked straight into his eyes and said, "Now."

Tobey was stunned. He was also struck dumb for the moment. After all his previous pondering and thinking about Eleanor's answer, he was not prepared for this immediate confirmation and the sudden rite of a marriage ceremony. None the less, he was pleased and finally uttered, "Very well."

Father John stood and clasped the hands of his sister and Tobey. "You know that you have my approval and blessing of this union, and it will be my distinct pleasure to perform the ceremony this morning. It will be more than special–my beloved sister and my first marriage to perform since I was ordained a priest. We will need to get some witnesses and we can proceed at once."

The bishop was away from his office, but Terry O'Shea was summoned as were two of the deacons assigned to the cathedral. The ceremony was to take place in Father John's office and not in the church nave. Tobey did not question any of the decisions made by the priest and his sister as he moved about in a state of shock over the rapidly unfolding events. He was certainly getting what he prayed for, and he reminded himself that it was well to be aware of what one prayed for because that is exactly what one received on many occasions.

The wedding party assembled and the bride and groom were directed to stand before the priest. The ceremony began.

When they came to the direct question, Father John said, "Do you Mary Eleanor Fitzpatrick, take Tobias Francis Boland to be your lawfully wedded husband?"

Eleanor did not answer. Tobey looked at Eleanor, then at Father John, who was looking at Eleanor.

Father John leaned over and whispered, "What's the matter, Sis, have you changed your mind?"

"That's not my name," hissed Eleanor.

Father John turned red, cleared his throat, and then said, "Do you Margaret Eleanor Fitzpatrick take Tobias Francis Boland to be your lawfully wedded husband?"

"I do," Eleanor replied in a loud firm voice.

And the wedding ceremony was done. Congratulations were offered by those present, and Father John brought out a bottle of wine and the newlyweds were toasted. It was not yet noon. Tobey was not certain what to do next now that he and Eleanor were married.

He turned to his new wife. "Would you like to take a trip somewhere? Perhaps to Cape Ann?"

Eleanor said, "No, my dear husband. The only trip I want to take is to my new home, our home. If you can have Terry stop the carriage at my lodging house and collect some of my belongings, I want to go straight to Worcester."

"That can be arranged, Mrs. Boland," Tobey said with a grin.

And before dark that day, June 25, 1841, the newly-wed couple arrived at Tobey's house.

Tobey's boys, though a bit restrained, were obviously pleased. The Irish domestics welcomed their new mistress with curtsies and smiles. And after the evening meal, Eleanor sat in the rocker by the fireplace and read to the children. Tobey sat in the opposite rocker and said a silent prayer of thanks. He realized a new chapter of his life was unfolding, and he believed it was going to be a good one.

On September 18, 1842, Eleanor went into labor. Although he now had arranged for doctors to attend the Irish community, Tobey always had fear in his heart about child birth. "Child birth fever" still took many of the Irish women as it had taken his Mary Ellen. Tobey paced the downstairs hall for hours eagerly waiting for a report from the upstairs bedroom. What was taking so long? With each passing hour, Tobey became more worried.

Finally, the doctor came down the stairs and said, "Congratulation, Mr. Boland. You have a son." He hesitated and a wave of fear came over Tobey. "In fact," the doctor continued, "You have two sons. Your wife has given birth to twin boys."

Tobey rushed up the stairs and into the bedroom. Eleanor was propped in the bed holding a baby in each arm.

"Two fine sons," she said. "And since we planned to name a son for my brother, we can still do that. Here we have John Bernard Fitzpatrick Boland and Thomas Bernard Fitzpatrick Boland. She looked from one baby to the other. "And in a dream," she said softly, "I have seen that one of them will become a priest."

Tobey nodded, greatly relieved that all three were in good health. When the new family members were more settled into the household, he turned his thoughts to more building and more creations–both human beings and physical structures.

CHAPTER FOURTEEN

Eleanor greeted Tobey at the front door of their home on his return from a week's trip inspecting and surveying various building operations of his construction company. He warmly embraced his wife and the two of them entered the house.

"There's good news," Tobey said. "I was able to get the twenty-two extra Patch acres at the auction today. Bishop Fenwick now has a total of seventy-four acres to present to the Jesuits for the proposed academy and if all goes well the seminary."

"I'm glad you were successful," Eleanor said. "After William Lincoln died, there was justifiable concern that the land might not be obtained."

"Well, that's settled now and what's more, the bishop directed me to go ahead and arrange for stone masons, brick makers, and carpenters, and order the supplies we will need for the upcoming building and have everything on hand in the spring. We'll add more buildings to the two I put up for Father Fitton. The bishop seems certain the Jesuits will approve the take over."

Tobey proceeded with the orders and soon supplies were being unloaded and stored all over the site. On April 25, Bishop Benedict Fenwick and Father John Fitzpatrick arrived for final inspection. With them were Tobey and Father Thomas Mulledy, S.J., former president of Georgetown and Provincial who had been assigned to supervise the construction of the new educational facility. He would head the new school and was now assigned to the diocese and living with the bishop in Boston.

On this day the group was to determine the precise building site. In May when Bishop Fenwick left for the Fifth Provincial Council of Baltimore, he left two thousand dollars to enable the project to proceed. On Sunday, June 13, he announced to his congregation in Boston the founding of The College of the Holy Cross in Worcester, named after his beloved Cathedral of the Holy Cross in Boston.

And finally the founding date for The College of the Holy Cross was declared June 13, 1843. The much anticipated day for the laying of the cornerstone arrived and a large crowd assembled. Tobey arranged for Eleanor and the older children to be present for this monumental occasion. The delegation from Boston arrived, coming by special train. Among that group were three men who were destined to become bishops–Father William Tyler, the first bishop of Hartford; Eleanor's brother, Father John Fitzpatrick who would become coadjutor to Bishop Fenwick and later the third bishop of Boston, and Father John McCloskey who would become Bishop of Albany and Archbishop of New York.

The day was beautiful, sunny and warm, with a slight breeze blowing across the crowd. Father Fitton's parishioners were present and a band played " Adeste Fidelis" and the popular "Hail Columbia." On the crest of Mount St. James, a cannon fired intermittently, shaking the ground beside it and sending smoke above the treetops and against the clear blue sky. Tobey's sons John and Frank were delighted and declared the cannon firing the highlight of the day.

Bishop Fenwick, adorned in all his bishop's finery, wearing his mitre and carrying his shepherd's crook, led the procession to a large wooden cross and the site of the corner stone. Into a solid block of granite a cavity was carved out and items were sealed into it--newspapers, coins, and a list with the names of President of the United States, John Tyler, and the governor of the Commonwealth of Massachusetts, Marcus Morton.

The bishop blessed the stone and said in Latin:

In the faith of Jesus Christ, we lay this first stone on the foundation in the name of the Father and of the Son and of the Holy Ghost, that true faith may flourish here, and the fear of God and fraternal affections; and may this place be devoted to involving and praising the name of our Lord Jesus Christ, Who, with the Father and the Holy Spirit, liveth and reigneth, one God, forever and ever.

As the builder in charge, Tobey tapped the stone into place with a wooden mallet, and the roar of the crowd was matched by the cannon firing again. Long and tiresome speeches followed and the speakers went on and on until finally Tobey and Eleanor retreated to the rear of the crowd with their restless children and sat on a hillside and ate a picnic lunch Eleanor had brought. Bridget, the Irish domestic, took charge of the children, so Tobey and Eleanor might continue to enjoy this wonderful day.

"I hope our sons can be among those educated here at The College of the Holy Cross," Tobey said.

"And our daughters as well," added Eleanor.

Her remark did not surprise Tobey at all. He nodded and smiled at his wife. “Stranger things have happened,” he said.

CHAPTER FIFTEEN

The Bolands traveled frequently between Worcester and Boston, for true to his promise, Tobey built a second home in the Roxbury area of Boston. He and Eleanor alternated their time between the two residences, and Tobey was busy with his construction business, going on many road trips in his sturdy carriage with faithful Terry O'Shea driving.

Eleanor continued to write columns for the Boston papers and some in New York. She still used the pen name "Alethe." When Tobey asked her why she choose that name, Eleanor replied that the alethe was a small bird that gathered bits of things and that she hoped her column could do as well with news items.

Her brother, Father John, was a frequent visitor to their home, and the Boland children grew very fond of "Uncle John" though they were constantly corrected to call him "Father John" especially when outside the house.

In March of 1844 Father John was called to Georgetown where he was made auxiliary bishop. Soon after that he became Bishop Coadjutor to Bishop Fenwick whose health was failing. On his return from the Georgetown trip, the new bishop came to visit Tobey and Eleanor who were at their Boston home at the time. He told them of meeting an interesting man, a prosperous planter named Michael Morris Healy, an Irish immigrant who had settled near Macon, Georgia and eventually acquired three thousand acres which he had planted in cotton. But, the Bishop continued, Michael had married a slave woman and had a close-knit family of ten children.

"He explained to me," Bishop John said, "That his children were classified as Negroes by the state of Georgia and thus were not allowed to receive any education. This was not at all satisfactory to Michael Healy and therefore, he sent the older children to the north where they had been receiving some schooling in New York. And now on a trip from Georgetown to New York, he had met Bishop Fitzpatrick. The purpose of this trip, he told the bishop, was to find a college for his oldest two boys, James and Hugh.

"Of course I suggested that he send them to Holy Cross," Father John said, "and I assured him that I and my family, meaning you, of course, would look after them."

John Fitzpatrick looked at Eleanor knowing what her reaction would be but also at Tobey about whom he was not so sure.

Eleanor smiled and said, "Of course we will look after them, won't we, Tobey?"

Tobey said nothing. He did nod his head in consent.

"And one more thing," the new bishop said. "I told him you two would be happy to have his twelve-year-old daughter, Martha, come and live with you."

"How wonderful to have a young girl in the house," Eleanor said at once.

"Yes," Tobey said. A strange way to get a daughter, he thought, but in the Boland household, there was always room for one more and a girl in the family would be a happy addition.

However, another female came to the Boland home and brought only sorrow and sadness. In 1845 Tobey and Eleanor experienced the heartbreak and tragedy of the death of their new-born daughter. A tiny baby girl called Ellen, the name Eleanor insisted on using, died a few days after she was born, and Tobey was pitched back into the memory and sorrow of the death of Elizabeth, his and Mary Ellen's first child.

Now death had claimed a second daughter, who joined Mary Ellen and baby Elizabeth in Tatnuck Cemetery.

With her strong faith in the will of God and the help of her brother the priest, Eleanor was able to handle the grief better than Tobey. While he remained silent in his thoughts, he had decided God did not intend for him to have a daughter of his own. He tried to console his grief with thoughts that it was a blessing that Eleanor had survived and maintained her good health.

As the Irish population was increasing, so the church was growing. On St. Patrick's Day in 1845, a foundation was laid for Christ's Church which would replace the wooden building Tobey had erected years before. The new structure would be dedicated with another name, St. John's. Tobey liked building churches as he thought he was building lasting contributions which did not go out of date as did canals.

Finally, the new year of 1846 brought happiness to Tobey and Eleanor who were blessed with a healthy baby daughter. She quickly grew into a strong young child, and although she was named Mary, she was always called Minnie by her older siblings, a name that lasted her lifetime. And Tobey at last felt very happy and blessed with his own little girl.

Tobey tried to remain at home more during this year with the new baby in the family, but he still had to travel a great deal in order to maintain his thriving construction business. He now had the reputation of being one of the finest contractors in the country and realized the wealth that such an occupation brought.

The College of the Holy Cross continued to grow. Bishop Fenwick turned the property over to the Jesuits on August 6, 1846. Five days later, this man, who had worked so hard for the establishment of the college, was given last rites by Bishop Fitzpatrick.

Bishop Fenwick died on August 11 and lay in state at The Cathedral of the Holy Cross in Boston. After a Requiem Mass, his body was moved to Worcester and on to the Holy Cross campus where he was buried in the spot he himself had picked out.

On March 27, 1847, the new east wing of the college opened and after classes, the students marched to the new chapel where they chanted the litanies.

The formal dedication of The College of the Holy Cross was held on April 22 when Bishop Fitzpatrick sang a solemn Requiem Mass for the repose of Bishop Fenwick's soul. The white marble memorial stone read,

"*Farewell, Beloved Bishop, be mindful of thy children.*"

Tobey always brought Eleanor the news he heard along the way in his travels. In the fall of 1845 Tobey told her of the report of a wide spread potato crop failure in Ireland and the many new problems of feeding people, most of whom were struggling with the harsh British rule which imposed devastating rents on the Irish people, and threw them out of their homes and off their land if payments were late.

"There is other food," Tobey said to Eleanor, "including corn and wheat, but the British are exporting those crops rather than feeding the hungry. They are more interested in profits and maintaining the economy than they are in feeding homeless and starving people. I fear this will lead to a crisis the likes of which Ireland has never seen before."

Within the next three years, the famine grew much worse and thousands of Irish left their native land and came to America where they hoped to find a place of dreams and promise. But many were soon disillusioned when they could not find work or living quarters. A chasm developed between the old established Irish and the newcomers who were angry to find so many of their fellow Irish living well in fine homes, enjoying a good life and acting and speaking more like Englishmen than Irishmen.

The new arrivals thought they were entitled to a similar good fortune, not realizing how hard it had been in the beginning for those who came to work on the Blackstone Canal. And Tobey was right in his prediction. Big trouble was brewing on the horizon.

CHAPTER SIXTEEN

Spring came early to Worcester in 1847 and railroad construction was continuing toward New Hampshire. Tobey held the contracts for this railroad work, but things were not going as well for his company as in the past. The newly arrived Irishmen were of a different sort. Most of them had fled the famine, and many came from the west side of the island and spoke only Gaelic. Most of them were also dependent on the "pioneer Irish" which is what Tobey's generation was being called. The new immigrants expected more of America, the Promised Land, than was available to them, and they expected those Irishmen who had come a quarter of a century earlier to take care of them with food, shelter, and jobs.

One Saturday Tobey rode with Terry O'Shea in his coach as they returned from the hiring fair that had taken place earlier in the day. They were discussing the many new problems they had incurred.

Terry spoke. "How were we to know that hundreds of Irish men would come storming into Worcester for the hiring fair, desperate for work? Where did they get the idea that thousands of jobs were available for the Providence and Worcester railroad?"

"They are desperate and beyond reasoning."

"These newly arrived Irishmen don't care about doing good work," Terry said, "In truth, they are not as skilled as our older workers, and the new fellows constantly complain. They seem to think they are entitled to everything. They have no idea the hardships we endured when we first got here to work on the Blackstone."

"I'm well aware of this," Tobey said. "That's our main reason for hiring the French Canadians to complete the Northern Nashua and Gardner line. They are much more dedicated to doing a good job."

"I know," Terry said, "and you know the two groups don't get along well at all. We try to keep them in separate crews, but the dissatisfaction spills beyond the work areas."

"We need the five hundred workers we hired today in order to take advantage of the summer weather," Tobey said, "But I'm distressed over the mood of the crowd when we closed the hiring fair. We could never have hired all those who were there."

Tobey looked out over the street as the carriage traveled on. Suddenly he stood and grabbed Terry on the shoulder. "Stop the coach!" he yelled. Terry pulled up the team, and Tobey jumped from the seat and began running down the road. Terry then saw what was happening.

Tobey's sons, John and Frank, were running along the road, followed closely by Bridget, the Boland domestic. And behind Bridget five or six rough looking men chased after them, waving their arms and yelling.

The men stopped when Tobey came between them and Bridget. Tobey turned to her.

"You and the boys get in the carriage," he said, then faced the mob. His blue eyes blazed with anger.

A man who appeared to be the mob leader called out. "Look, boys, it's Lord Normansby himself. Let's get him." The man began to move toward Tobey.

Tobey braced for an attack, but Terry pulled the carriage along beside Tobey. The children and Bridget had already leaped inside the cabin.

"Get in, Boss," Terry cried out. "There's too many of them. Let's get out of here."

Tobey surveyed the situation and decided Terry was right. He hopped onto the step of the coach, and Terry cracked the whip over the heads of the horses and headed straight toward the crowd. They jumped aside and the carriage sped on down the road. Tobey moved up to the seat by Terry again.

"They're going too far now," Tobey said, breathing heavily. "We have to do something about this."

Once they were safely at home, Tobey questioned the boys and Bridget.

"We were just playing," John said, "And this man came up and tried to grab me. He said he would give me some sweets, but I didn't believe he had any. I ran and I yelled to Frank to run."

"You did the smart thing, and the right thing," Tobey said.

"I don't think they knew I was with the boys," Bridget said. Her eyes were wide open and she still looked frightened. "I got between the men and the boys and started to run, too. I was ever so glad to see your coach coming down the road."

"You and the boys go on inside," Tobey said. "Terry, tend to the horses, but don't put them away. We may be going out again."

"What's the matter?" Eleanor had come to the front door when she heard the commotion.

Tobey came into the house and explained what had just occurred.

"Thank God you came upon them when you did," Eleanor said. "Did they follow you home?"

"I don't think so," Tobey said, and waved Eleanor to a chair in the parlor. "We have to discuss this and take some action."

Eleanor sat beside Tobey and waited to see what he planned to do.

"I want you to take the children and Bridget and go to Boston tonight," Tobey said.

"But tomorrow is Palm Sunday and the beginning of Holy Week," Eleanor said.

"I realize that, but seeing that group this afternoon makes me think there are far too many of these transients who are stirred up and looking to cause trouble. They were at a boiling point at the hiring fair this morning. Those scum who chased the boys even called me Lord Normansby."

"Lord Normansby! That awful English landlord who has treated the Irish so poorly and thrown them out of their homes and off their land?"

"That very one." Tobey said. "Now do as I say and go get yourself and the children ready to leave for Boston right now."

"But what will you do?" Eleanor now showed alarm.

"I'll have Terry come back and get me first thing in the morning. You prefer Boston to Worcester anyway and things need to calm down here. You can see your brother and attend Palm Sunday services at the cathedral."

Eleanor was not a woman to be ordered around, but neither was she unreasonable. She had heard tales of the unrest and conflict among the newly arrived Irishmen and those who had been established in

Worcester many years. And she trusted Tobey's judgment in this matter.

Tobey instructed Terry to take the family to the Boston house and return for him as soon as possible Sunday morning. He helped load them into the crowded cab of the coach and then waved goodbye to his family as the coach moved east toward Boston.

CHAPTER SEVENTEEN

Palm Sunday dawned as clear and as warm as the previous day. Before the sun had come completely over the eastern skyline, Tobey was climbing into his coach. Out of concern for his mentor, Terry had driven the four hours back late the night before, slept a few hours and let the horses rest. Now he and Tobey were off again.

As Tobey and Terry made their way out of Worcester, the streets of Irish Shanty Town in the Meadows began to teem with people–the regular residents, those visiting them for Holy Week, and those who had come to town for the hiring fair milled about all day and filled the taverns, most of which were drunk dry by afternoon.

As the sun was beginning to go down, a large mob approached Donlevie's tavern, only to find it had closed. The angry and thirsty crowd called the owner out and demanded he open the bar. Over his protests that he had no liquor in the place, they pushed forward, broke in, and began to smash everything within reach, but they found nothing to quench their thirst.

Someone shouted there was liquor to be had at the brewery on Grafton Street and the angry crowd moved in that direction. A lone watchman at the brewery calmly told them there was no drink stored there on a weekend, so the mob pushed on down Water Street on the east bank of the canal throwing rocks and bottles, breaking windows and pushing down fences. They crossed the Madison Street Bridge into Scalpintown, the quiet neighborhood where most of the old established "lace curtain" Irish lived.

Small groups broke off down alleys, but the main body of the mob headed toward Tobey's "Castle," as they called it, on Green Street.

"We want Lord Normansby," they shouted.

"Where is the Saxon tyrant?"

"He promised us jobs at the hiring fair and didn't give us any."

"He gave our jobs to the Canadians."

They soon reached Tobey's house, only to be disappointed. All was dark. Tobey and his family had wisely left town.

But the mob was not satisfied. They moved on down Temple Street toward the second target of their rage, the Reverend Matthew Gibson, pastor of St. John's Church.

The priest was eating his dinner when the mob stormed up on the porch of the rectory, and began banging on the door and shouting. Gibson thought he could calm the crowd by going on the front porch and speaking to them. He was wrong.

The mob dragged him into the street and called him "the Landlord's Priest," pounded him with their fists and threw him to the ground. Then they ignored him and began to break windows in the rectory. Father Gibson scurried inside and brought out tools and boards, and he and the household servants tried to nail them across the windows and doors. But the crowd of angry men still lingered on the porch and in the street. They yelled threats at the priest again, and Father Gibson finally scrambled into the house and out the back door of the rectory and fled to the home of a neighbor.

"Come in, come in," the neighbor said. "Are you hurt?"

"Not badly, but those men mean to kill me," Father Gibson said. His voice was trembling and he was shaking. "Can you get me to the depot? I'm leaving here."

A short time later, under cover of darkness, the two men slipped out of the house and went in the direction away from the mob, which was still throwing rocks at the rectory and shouting, "English tyrant."

Father Gibson took the night train to Boston.

When Tobey arrived in Boston, he and Eleanor met with Bishop Fitzpatrick, who was upset over the Palm Sunday riot. The clergyman had always believed in law and order and reason, all missing in the Palm Sunday riots in Worcester.

"There are so many factors to blame," the bishop said. "First, I had my doubts when Bishop Fenwick appointed Father Gibson to St. John's. Being so very English, he was from the beginning a misfit with the Irish, with his fancy vestments and his takeover of so many duties the parishioners had been handling themselves for the church for so long."

"And he went along with them in firing me from supervising the St. John's Church construction right in the middle of the building," Tobey said with anger in his voice.

"That was an unfortunate move," Bishop Fitzpatrick said, "but there were so many other factors. Too many of the newcomers are from the west of Ireland, while the established Irish came from the eastern part. Those two sides differ in more than language, and things have gotten so out of reason that those who have fled the famine seem to blame the people in America for the failure of the potato crop and the desperate situation in Ireland.

"I instructed Father Gibson to investigate the charges made by the Shamrock Society about exploitation by leaders and shopkeepers, but he only condemned the Society in public which was a big mistake in judgment. That made them even angrier, and sent the Shamrocks underground where they are now more difficult to deal with."

"The parish seemed more receptive when Father John Boyce came as co-pastor," Eleanor said. "Perhaps he will be able to restore some order in the activities of St. John's."

Bishop Fitzpatrick nodded and murmured, "God willing."

"Let's hope so," Tobey said, "But in the meantime, Eleanor, I want you and the children to remain here in Boston. Easter is this Sunday, and we can't risk putting you and the family in harm's way again."

And so Eleanor and the children and the domestics remained in the Boston house the remainder of the year. Two significant events took place in 1848 while the family lived in the Boston residence.

Another son, this one named Benjamin, was born with both mother and child in good health. But Tobey's first American achievement, the Blackstone Canal, closed forever just as he had predicted it would. Even though Tobey had foreseen the demise of the Blackstone the day it had opened, he was saddened to learn it had ceased operation.

"The shareholders never received a dollar of return on their investment," he said to Eleanor. "And they never will. Railroads are now all over New England, many of them built by my own company."

"I'm thankful your business continues to grow and bring you such a fine reputation and us a steady income," Eleanor said.

"I'd say it depends on who you ask about the fine reputation," Tobey smiled, "I was not very popular with that Palm Sunday crowd. Nevertheless, with the family growing like it is, we need the income to feed us all. And, I expect we'll have an even larger crowd and a house full for the coming Christmas season."

As the year 1848 drew to a close, it appeared Christmas would be a happier time. And indeed it was.

Snow had blanketed the city in white and on Christmas Eve, which fell on a Sunday, James Healy arrived from Holy Cross College to spend the holidays with the Bolands and his sister, who was still living with them. The student from Georgia was now a senior at the college, and though he had told no one so far, he was having thoughts about entering the priesthood. He hoped his visit with the Boland family would give him the opportunity to talk about his intentions with his great friend and benefactor, Bishop Fitzpatrick.

All the family and guests attended Christmas Eve Mass at St. John's Church in East Cambridge, and after supper the Bolands and their friends sat up late talking about the next day and preparing Christmas presents and stockings.

After they attended an early Mass Christmas morning, there was a festive Boland eggnog party in celebration of the holiday. Later in the day James and his sister, Martha, went to The Cathedral of the Holy Cross where James followed the pontifical Mass from the sacristy, marveling at the choir's rendition of Haydn's ***Christmas Mass*** and wondering if he would ever be standing before the altar as a celebrant.

Bishop John Fitzpatrick and two other priests came to the Boland home Christmas night for supper, and all shared in Christmas games with the children. While playing the Christmas Bag game, Thomas Boland took a big swing with his cane and nearly hit the bishop in the head. Fortunately, James Healy caught the wild swing and later James broke the string and the bag and ended the game before any more sticks endangered the clergy.

"Play the piano for us," the children urged the bishop.

"I'm too rusty," the bishop said. "I haven't played the piano in a long time."

"Do play, John," Eleanor said. "We would all love to sing along with some Christmas carols."

Bishop John Bernard Fitzpatrick sat down at the piano and began to play a few chords. Soon the entire group was singing

"Listen to this one," the bishop said and he sang a solo in German called ***Stille Nicht***.

"What a lovely melody," Eleanor said.

"It is beautiful, isn't it?" Bishop John said, and he told them how this Christmas carol had been written in Oberndorf, a small Austrian town with a guitar as accompaniment because the organ in the little church was broken. "One day maybe someone will publish it in English," he said, "And it will become a well loved American Christmas carol."

Tobey, his family, and the visitors enjoyed time together in the days after Christmas. The winter weather, as always, had shut down all construction and building for Tobey's company and work crews.

James Healy stayed several more days and one morning he headed for the cathedral stating that he was going to talk to the bishop.

As he disappeared down the walkway, Eleanor turned to Tobey. "He's going into the priesthood," she said.

"How do you know that?" Tobey asked.

"Trust me," Eleanor smiled. "I can always tell."

CHAPTER EIGHTEEN

Early in 1850 another son was born to Tobey and Eleanor. The new boy, who would be their last child, was named Leo Paul. Tobey's oldest sons by his first wife, John and Frank, were now seventeen and fifteen years of age and Tobey was including them in his business matters more often. Both young men seemed to have inherited their father's natural instinct for building, and they enjoyed traveling with their father and learning about construction.

Eleanor wrote her "Alethe" magazine and newspaper columns, addressing some of the pressing problems of the day. These writings were being published in Boston and New York publications. On occasion, Eleanor made some comment on politics, and she brought up the matter of women's rights more than once. She taught some classes in the Boston schools because there was a shortage of Greek and Latin teachers, but the growing family restricted her activities outside the home.

Tobey was not at all surprised, however, when in late summer, Eleanor announced that she was going to Worcester to attend the first National Women's Rights Convention to be held October 23 and 24. From the days before their marriage, Tobey had always known that Eleanor "had a mind of her own" as her brother had phrased it, and Tobey learned more of her firm disposition and convictions every day. He took pride, however, in her keen intellect and her ability to analyze problems and solve them. In the nine years since they had been married, he had increased his admiration for this unusual woman and her devotion to him and to their children as well as to her step-children. He remembered she had questioned him about love for her. He knew now that he could answer that question. She was an inspiration and a light in his life. And whatever Eleanor wanted, Tobey would get it for her if it was humanly possible.

He would never have attempted to prevent her from attending this Women's Rights Convention, but he did have unspoken reservations about her going because of the great controversy it was creating. There was fierce opposition to the convention from all sides. Some newspapers were calling the supporters and the attendees "fanatics and lunatics." ***The New York Herald*** wrote that the delegates in Worcester were "gloomy and warlike" in appearance. A great issue was made over the fact that there were no babies present. Eleanor commented that no woman in her right mind would bring a child, let alone a baby, to such a gathering, and she added that presenting such an argument only reflected on the ignorance of those speakers.

"Why is it men are never questioned about bringing children into business meetings?" Eleanor asked.

When the National Women's Rights Convention opened, over 1000 delegates from eleven states had arrived for the gathering. Eleanor offered the hospitality of the Bolands' Worcester house to many of the women attending, and there they continued their discussions into the night.

Some of the featured speakers were Lucretia Mott, Lucy Stone, Abby Kelley Foster, wife of Stephen S. Foster of musical fame, and Sarah H. Earle, wife of John Milton Earle, editor of the local newspaper, ***The Worcester Spy***. Several men were among the speakers. ***The Spy*** ran an article which commented on the forensic talent and speaking ability presented by the female speakers who were quite professional in their oratory skills.

A rare woman physician was present on the platform, Harriet K. Hunt, whose address stressed the importance of women becoming doctors and the need for schools to train them. She did not ask for "separate but equal" medical schools for women, but rather that they be afforded the opportunity to attend the existing institutions along with the men.

A major issue at the Worcester convention, one that would rage for years to come, was women's suffrage. Speaker after speaker addressed the issue. They bristled at the accusation that women were not capable of casting intelligent ballots. "If we are capable," they said, "of bringing the next generation into the world, we can certainly cast votes as to the direction that world should take."

"Every drunk in a barroom brawl can vote, but that right is denied women," Eleanor said to a group gathered at her home the night the convention closed. "We have to change that, along with allowing women to own property, especially when they bring their own into a marriage. And certainly any wages earned by a woman should be hers and not automatically given to her husband."

But opposition continued loud and angry even after the meeting closed. The delegates were often accused of trying to make themselves into men. The American Anti-Slavery Society was caught in the middle because many Abolitionists were not willing to give a woman the same rights they were demanding for male slaves.

"They want to free the slaves but leave half the population in bondage," Eleanor said to Tobey the night she returned from the meeting.

"You really have strong feelings about this, don't you?" Tobey said.

"Yes, I do," Eleanor answered. "First I could never become a priest because of my gender. Well, now I am determined to assume the responsibilities of fighting for equal rights, voting rights, and some rights for women who are forced to do factory work."

"Do you still wish you could have been a priest?" Tobey asked quietly. Eleanor turned her dark brown eyes and looked deeply into the sky-blue eyes of Tobey Boland.

She got up and walked across the room and put her hand on his shoulder. "No, dear Tobey," she said. "I no longer wish to be a priest. I would much rather be your wife and mother to our children."

Tobey grasped both her hands in his. "You once asked me if I would love you," he said. "Never more than I do at this very minute. You are the greatest blessing of my life."

CHAPTER NINETEEN

On a summer afternoon in July, 1852, Bishop John Fitzpatrick traveled to Worcester to St. John's Church where Father Matthew Gibson was still priest in charge. Things had quieted since the Palm Sunday riots and the bishop had decided not to move Father Gibson from the parish.

The two men were enjoying lunch together, and Bishop Fitzpatrick was bragging on James Healy who had finished as valedictorian in the first graduating class at Holy Cross in 1849.

"He is going to make a fine priest," the bishop said. "There was a bit of a problem establishing his birth certificate in Georgia, but that has been settled. In fact I am thinking of bringing him into the diocesan headquarters to assist in a number of ways."

"I have not met the young man," Father Gibson said, "but if he meets with your approval, he must be a good choice."

"What's that?" Father Gibson rose from the table and went to the window that overlooked the street.

"Father, Father," shouted a boy below. "The Catholic College is on fire!"

The two clergymen leaped up and hurried to the top floor of the rectory, and to their horror, saw billowing smoke and flames pouring from the top floor of the main Holy Cross building.

"Let's get out there at once," the bishop said, and they joined the large crowd moving toward Mount St. James. A fire engine raced ahead of them.

They found confusion and chaos. While the fire roared and spread, the fireman discovered there was an inadequate supply of water; and they were pulling hoses to the Blackstone River in a vain struggle to get sufficient water to put out the towering flames and preserve as much as possible of the Holy Cross property.

Books, personal belongings, and furnishings were scattered over the ground where they had been thrown from floors above in an attempt to save some things. Despite their heroic efforts, the fireman, students, and townspeople were not able to save the building. Nothing was left standing except the east wing which contained the study hall, refectory, and a chapel. Fortunately, the library, scientific apparatus and some furniture had not burned.

Tears glistened in the eyes of Bishop Fitzpatrick as he looked at Father Gibson. "We have no insurance on this property," he said sadly. "But by the grace of God, we will preserve this College of the Holy Cross. It shall not perish."

Only the dedication and determination of Bishop John Bernard Fitzpatrick with building knowledge and financial assistance from his brother-in-law, Tobias Boland, kept The College of the Holy Cross from dying in the ashes of the tragic fire.

The blaze had apparently started when a teacher was burning old exam papers in a third floor stove on that hot July day. With debts but no insurance and no funds on hand, The Rev. Joseph Aschwanden, acting head of the Maryland Province which had jurisdiction over Jesuit activities in New England, immediately let it be known that the Jesuits wanted no part in rebuilding the college.

But the citizens of the whole community rallied behind rebuilding the college. Some offered rooms to faculty and students at no charge. The Rev. Anthony F. Ciampi, S.J., the new college president, wrote a stern letter. Defending Holy Cross College against the institutions to the south, he stated that he "found more life in the ruins of Worcester than in the whole of Maryland."

When Father Aschwanden offered to transfer the college, including its $12.000 debt, back to Bishop Fitzpatrick, the offer was flatly refused. The bishop said it would be a breach of faith and a black mark on the memory of Bishop Fenwick.

Bishop Fitzpatrick prevailed with the help of the Holy Cross community and the people of Worcester. Donations came from rich and poor, from Catholics and Protestants. James Healy's brother, Patrick Healy, donated $2300 at a critical time.

In his own way, Tobey worked as hard as the bishop and devoted many hours to the re-building of the college. He supported his brother-in-law in every possible way--financially, physically, spiritually, and emotionally.

"It would seem," Tobey said on one occasion, "That brothers-in-law are destined to play an important role in my life."

Eleanor kept up with the progress. "It should be remembered that Holy Cross has given twelve vocations to the Jesuits, while there have been only three from Georgetown."

"We can always count on you to keep up with the number of newly ordained priests," Tobey said, smiling as he spoke.

Finally on April 4, 1853, it was confirmed that Holy Cross would be rebuilt and reopened. The fee for tuition, room and board was raised from $150 to $170, and classes resumed on October 3, 1853.

CHAPTER TWENTY

Tobey's oldest son John was working with Tobey and Michael Callahan on many construction projects. This son was called "Big John" so he would not be confused with the twin named John Bernard Fitzpatrick Boland who was called "Twin John."

Big John was full of adventure and argued with Tobey to let him go to California. Since gold had been discovered there in 1849, Big John had a burning desire to join the gold rush.

"There's more gold in construction," Tobey told him. "By the time you could get out there, all the gold will have been dug up or panned out of the streams. It's 190 days by boat, and overland is unthinkable."

Tobey promoted Big John to second-in-command under Michael Callahan and sent the two of them to Canada on one of the large new contracts Tobey had obtained in that country. The other twin, Thomas, was then allowed to travel some with his father. Twin John was spending more and more time with his uncle, the bishop, always doing some job at the cathedral.

When Tobey questioned Eleanor about her ability to spot one heading for the priesthood, she nodded and said, "Yes, I think our son Twin John will become a priest as soon as he is old enough to be admitted to the program."

Tobey had never been particularly interested in politics, but in the construction business, he could not avoid dealing with certain aspects of the government and its workings.

In the 1854 election in Massachusetts, the Whigs, who had dominated politics in the state for a quarter of a century, were ousted by the new American Party, better known as the "Know Nothing" party, great advocates of religious and racial discrimination. The long-held discrimination against the Irish was still very much a part of Irish life and was intensified by the large number of Irishmen who had fled the famine in their homeland and now lived in the Worcester area. The newcomers were untrained, poor, and unqualified for work other than construction jobs. They were restless and in a great hurry to better themselves in any way they could.

Eleanor was livid about the Know Nothing Party. "All they can say is 'we know nothing', and that is the absolute truth. They certainly are ignorant, and they have passed some of the most biased and ridiculous laws ever enacted. The directive that the common King James English version of the Bible be read in all school classes daily is an attempt to discredit the Catholic Bible," she said to Tobey. "And this Nunnery Committee asking for a law to inspect all convents and nunneries and other Catholic institutions is an invasion of the rights of citizens."

"Worse than that," Tobey said. "Much worse than that. Such a committee has already been sent to inspect Holy Cross College, with the expense charged to the tax-paying citizens of this state. The group inspecting said they were looking for treason, proselytism and subversive activity."

"And what did they find?" Eleanor asked, her dark eyes flashing.

"Nothing of course," Tobey said, "And the story goes that they left the campus and spent half the night in riotous drinking in a local tavern with ladies of the night." He laughed.

"It isn't funny," Eleanor said "We have to get the Know Nothings out of office. Now, if the women had the franchise, that awful party would be voted out in a heartbeat."

"I've done what I could by supporting the Democrats in the recent elections," Tobey said. "Maybe that will pay off for us."

And pay off it did. A few days later, Tobey came home and announced to Eleanor that they had both been invited to the White House by the recently elected President Franklin Pierce, who at 48 years of age, was the youngest ever elected to the presidency.

"You will remember Pierce is from New Hampshire and a staunch Democrat who won by a landside over the Whigs, thanks in a great part to our Irish Catholic support. He has called a meeting of contractors and builders in Washington with the idea of discussing and setting up some National Programs. Would you like to go to Washington?"

Eleanor thought over what Tobey said. "Yes, definitely. This is a startling new concept to have wives invited to the White House. Yes, I'd like to go. Do accept the invitation."

"Wives should add to the experience, although I hear Pierce's wife does not participate in any presidential affairs. We probably won't even see her. They have lost all three of their sons, two in infancy and one in a terrible accident. This was before Pierce was elected, and the word is that his wife is not participating in any social events at all."

"How heart breaking," Eleanor said, "Her reaction is understandable."

Eleanor and Tobey made the trip from Boston to Washington by ship. Tobey moved with caution, ever aware of his tendency to sea sickness, but Eleanor roamed the decks, leaned into the wind and let the waves spray the ocean mist into her face. She enjoyed every minute of the sea voyage.

Tobey was amazed at the changes and developments which had taken place since his last visit to Washington. The Bolands had a splendid time in the nation's capital, and reveled in their visit to the White House with all the dignitaries gathered. Tobey returned to Boston with the title of Director of Customs for the Port of Boston.

"Not exactly a building contract," he said to Eleanor when the announcement was made. "But it can't hurt to be in the position to participate and do business with the commerce of the port."

Tobey moved into his new position with enthusiasm and soon learned much about imports and exports and about shipping.

As was his habit, he brought the news of the day home to share and discuss with Eleanor each night.

"I'm not sure how much longer President Pierce will have any influence in politics," Tobey said. "He is angering many of his supporters, and I think he has killed any chance of being elected to a second term. He's now come out in favor of the Kansas-Nebraska Act, repealing the Missouri Compromise which will reopen the question of expansion of slavery in the west."

Eleanor frowned. "We are fast headed to a showdown regarding the slavery issue, aren't we?" she said. "I greatly fear it will tear this country apart."

CHAPTER TWENTY-ONE

Bishop Fitzpatrick was still a frequent visitor in the Boland home. Although he looked hearty, he had not been well since he had suffered what appeared to be a minor stroke. He was ordered by his doctors to take a long rest to recover from what they termed "cerebral congestion." The man who worked tirelessly and was in every aspect the life of his diocese was advised to engage in only the lightest sort of concentrated and administrative work. He transferred even more duties to the Rev. James Sealy, who now became a constant companion with Bishop John, lightening his clerical load by accompanying him on confirmation excursions, parish visits, inspections and formal church occasions as well as handling many of the administrative duties of the bishop's office.

The two were a study in contrast. Bishop John was tall and well proportioned, and moved with all the stately dignity his high office afforded. Father James was of slight stature, though erect and military-like in his bearing. In contrast to the Bishop's receding hairline, Father James had a full head of hair. The two often welcomed boatloads of immigrants at the wharf in Boston with an Irish brogue, offering a warm and friendly Catholic welcome to the newcomers. It was a strong contrast to the inhospitable greetings directed toward earlier Irish settlers in Massachusetts.

While the doctor's orders may have slowed Bishop Fitzpatrick down in his physical work, he never let go of his high dreams for the future. He spoke often to Tobey about his plan for a new and glorious Gothic Cathedral to replace the old Cathedral of the Holy Cross which was no longer large enough. Bishop John had even engaged an architect, Patrick Keeley, to draw up plans for an American Gothic cathedral to rival the splendid ones in Europe and, he hoped, be even more beautiful than Notre Dame in Paris.

"You know we have to have a larger cathedral," the bishop said to Tobey. "And I want it to be the grandest Glory to God in America."

"It would be well to consider that this country may soon be in a war over this issue of slavery and states' rights," Tobey said.

"Let us pray not," the bishop said. "I am scheduling a Mass for maintaining the unity of the Union to be said very soon. We must pray for a peaceful solution."

"Unity will be hard to achieve when large economic issues are at stake," Tobey said. "But you are right that we must pray for a peaceful solution."

But the bishop was certain that his dream for the new cathedral would be realized in his life time, and he went ahead with the plans for selling the old cathedral building. In September of 1860 the building was sold to Isaac Rich for one hundred and thirty thousand dollars. Sunday, September 16, arrived quickly and the last Mass in the old cathedral was celebrated.

Tobey and Eleanor sat in their usual pew with the children as Bishop John celebrated a Solemn Pontifical High Mass. When it came time for the sermon, the last address that Bishop Fitzpatrick would ever make from the old Cathedral of the Holy Cross, the congregation was startled to see the Rev. James Healy take the pulpit. He proceeded to read the sermon notes the bishop had given him.

Eleanor was alarmed and whispered to Tobey, "Where is John? Has he been taken ill?"

Tobey pointed out that her brother was sitting in his bishop's chair dabbing at his eyes. Only later did they learn that Bishop John Fitzpatrick was so emotionally overcome at leaving the cathedral where he had served most of his ministry that he could not make his last remarks and had asked James Healy to take over.

CHAPTER TWENTY-TWO

The old Cathedral of the Holy Cross in Boston was torn down immediately and soon there was only a vacant lot where the old church had served so long. But before a brick could be laid for the new cathedral, Rebel guns fired on Fort Sumter and South Carolina withdrew from the United States. Other Southern states followed, and the country was plunged into a bloody war that lasted four years and tore the United States of America into a long-lasting disaster.

Tobey's prediction about the conflict between the northern and southern states having a great effect on the economy had come from his astute sense of business. And he was right. Everything was affected, not just construction, but finances, banking, commerce, manufacturing, and most especially the people and society as a whole.

The conflict, which some had expected to be over in a matter of months, began to escalate as the Union army floundered, losing battle after battle. Amid a sea of controversy, Abraham Lincoln was elected president. Everything was now directed to the war effort and the economy. The South still insisted on its right to withdraw from the Union. The slavery issue, which was affecting the agricultural economy of the Confederate States, became a battle as intense as the conflicts of the armies.

The Union army needed more troops. Conscription was enacted into law, only to have the wealthy buy their way out of army service. By paying $300 or engaging a substitute, wealthier young men did not have to enlist, creating what some called "the rich man's war fought by the poor man."

Hundreds of Irish workers found themselves with no construction jobs, so they began to take advantage of the money they could make by joining the Union army and by hiring themselves out to take the place of the privileged. Measured by their military service, the Irish showed more loyalty to their new country than those who had long lived in America.

The Irish, however, were not necessarily in favor of abolishing slavery, for they feared their jobs would be lost to newly freed black workers pouring in from the plantations of the South.

Tobey made what adjustments he could among those who worked for him, but there were few contracts for regular construction. The war effort took priority with manufacture of arms, weapons, and military supplies.

Tobey told Eleanor he expected Big John to return from Canada any day to enlist in the Union army.

"I don't want to see him go to into battle, but it's the kind of adventure Big John will relish," Tobey said.

But it was not Big John who came back to Boston, but Michael Callahan, and Michael was alone.

"God bless all in this house," Michael blurted out as he came into the Boland home.

Tobey greeted his long time assistant and looked over Michael's shoulder.

"But where is Big John?" Tobey asked.

Michael shuffled his feet and hung his head. Suddenly the big husky foreman burst into tears.

"I had to come and tell you meself," he sobbed. "I couldn't send the word, and I couldn't use that new fangled telegraph."

Tobey felt a great jolt of fear and he took Michael by the shoulders. "What is it, Michael? Where is John?"

"Big John, he–Big John is gone—it was a black powder explosion on our job. He's gone. I wanted to bring him home to you," Michael tried to finish, "but you have to believe it was best to bury him in Canada. I'm so sorry, Tobey. You sent me with him to take care of him and–and--I have failed you. And I failed him."

Michael's shoulders shook. The big Irishman sat heavily in a chair and put his face in his hands and continued to sob.

Tobey stood stiff and rigid. He could not, he would not believe what Michael was telling him. It was not possible that his wonderful grown son was to join the other children that death had taken from him. This was just a bad dream, a nightmare, and soon he would wake up. His mind raced in denial and disbelief. He would not, he could not, accept this news. After a long pause, he walked over where Michael sat and put his hand on Michael's shoulder.

"Don't blame yourself," Tobey said. "We've always known how dangerous black powder was--and is."

He crossed the room to a sideboard and mechanically took a bottle of Irish whiskey and poured it into two large glasses. One he handed to Michael. He took a large gulp from the other.

Eleanor appeared at the doorway. She knew instinctively that something was dreadfully wrong.

Tobey looked at his wife. "How many more of my children will death steal from me?" he asked. "I had such plans for Big John to take over the business, and now--and now, he's gone, too."

Tobey saw the look of shock on her face and realized Eleanor did not know what he was talking about. He could not bring himself to say that Big John was dead.

And so he said, "Our children should outlive us. That's the natural order of life. We aren't supposed to bury them."

Eleanor crossed the room and put her arms around Tobey. Finally she said, "What happened?"

Tobey took a deep breath and said, "Construction accident–black powder explosion."

Eleanor took the glass from Toby's fingers and put it on the sideboard. She continued to hold him tightly as he stared into space.

"To be Irish is to know," Tobey whispered, "that in the end the world will break your heart."

Finally, racking sobs and tears came to Tobey.

Eleanor stroked his shoulder. "I'll get in touch with the bishop for a requiem Mass," she said.

CHAPTER TWENTY-THREE

Now in his sixties, Tobey had to face the departure of his next son. Frank had spent considerable time with Tobey at the Boston Customs Office, where he became fascinated with ships and matters of the sea.

Tobey was not surprised when one day Frank announced his intention to contribute to the war effort.

"I'm going to join the U.S. Navy," Frank said to his father. "The military is going to be coming after me, and I don't want to be in the army."

"I know you must have to serve soon," Tobey said. "I would rather you be with the navy than a foot soldier." In his heart he dreaded Frank's departure, and so Tobey tried to make light of the conversation by adding, "I hope you do not suffer your father's tendency to sea sickness."

All too soon Frank's ship sailed from Boston Harbor and out of sight on the horizon. Tobey stood for a long time on the pier staring after it, wondering if he would ever see his son Frank again. "Don't take him too. Please let Frank live," Tobey whispered to the gently cresting waves.

The conflict for the preservation of the Union went on with bloody battle after bloody battle taking place across the country. More and more troops were added to the army of the Union. Recently elected President Lincoln kept changing the Union generals, but nothing seemed to improve the war effort.

Early in 1862 Bishop Fitzpatrick announced that he was going to Europe to try and regain his health. While he didn't doubt his brother-in-law was in need of medical rest, Tobey thought there was another reason for the trip. After Bishop Fitzpatrick had arrived on the continent, Tobey talked to Eleanor about it.

"He barely stopped at the Vatican and didn't linger long in Italy," Tobey said, "And now Bishop John is staying at the United States legation in Brussels. Is he there on behalf of President Lincoln to build up better relations with those Catholic nations of Europe that are sympathetic to the Confederacy?"

"I can't answer that," Eleanor said. "You know how close John and I have always been, but he did not choose to reveal to me any reason other than that he was traveling to Europe for his health. The decline in his physical condition is of great concern to me. I pray constantly for improvement in his health."

Tobey persisted. "Archbishop John Hughes of New York is working in France for the Union cause. It's logical that your brother is doing the same in Belgium."

"If it will help end this awful war, then it is a good thing," Eleanor said.

Tobey decided to say nothing to Eleanor later when he heard that the United States consul, Henry Sanford, had reported to Secretary of State William Seward that Bishop Fitzpatrick had "strengthened our cause; and done a great deal to project a much more favorable image of the Union point of view."

On January 1, 1863 Lincoln issued The Emancipation Proclamation freeing the slaves. This was received in the Northern states with optimism and celebration, but some, especially Irish Catholics, were not pleased and saw it only as impending disaster. They no longer supported Lincoln or his administration.

Tobey had long ago decided to observe rather than participate in this debate.

A bloody three-day civil rampage broke out in New York City in July with demonstrations and riots so severe that Union army troops had to be brought in from the Gettysburg campaign to restore order.

With Bishop Fitzpatrick still in Europe, it fell to Father James Healy to take measures to prevent the same sort of unrest occurring in Boston.

"I know Bishop John would never condone violence in any form," Father James said to Tobey. "His recourse has always been legal and constitutional solution."

"The mayor's quick action in calling in city police and the local militia has contained the initial outbreaks," Tobey said.

"Yes, and I intend to get out a letter to the clergy asking that they take an active part in suppressing problems. I will ask them to patrol the streets and tell people to stay inside their homes and avoid any group protesting."

"The bishop may be far away, but he will condone your actions and concur with them," Tobey said.

In 1864 Eleanor received word that Bishop Fitzpatrick was returning from Europe. Father Healy had heard also and went to meet the ship in Halifax where it stopped to refuel. Father Healy was distressed to see the physical condition of his mentor after the rough north Atlantic crossing.

Eleanor and daughter Minnie were at the rectory in Boston when the bishop arrived. She, too, was distraught at his physical deterioration. He was limping and dragging his left side which had been affected by his earlier stroke. An icy fear gripped her heart as she realized how gravely ill her beloved brother was.

Parades and celebration erupted on Sunday April 9, 1865 when the news arrived that General Robert E. Lee had surrendered to General Ulysses S. Grant at Appomattox. The jubilation of the armistice quickly fell into gloom when, on Good Friday, President Abraham Lincoln was shot while attending a play at Ford's Theater in Washington. He died early the next morning.

Bishop Fitzpatrick was not physically able to celebrate any Mass so Father Healy presided at the High Mass on Easter Sunday and read Bishop John's decree that all Catholic churches participate in mourning by holding services of a penitential nature at the same time of the official Protestant observance on the day of the funeral.

Bishop Fitzpatrick made only a few official appearances, and by December he was confined to bed in his room at the rectory. Father Healy set up an altar so Mass could be said there.

The man of logic and reason held an optimistic attitude and still kept a log of his daily thoughts, but on December 13, he suffered a severe and prolonged hemorrhage. On December 20 he signed his last will and testament.

Eleanor did her best to keep up a positive composure, but she confessed her distress to Tobey.

"I cannot bear the thought of losing John," she said. "He is only fifty-three years old and he has so much to offer to the world. How can God possibly take him from us?"

And it seemed Eleanor's prayers were answered, at least temporarily, for the bishop's condition improved by Christmas Day. She went to visit him at his bedside.

Taking his hand, she said, "You are so much better."

But Bishop John looked into the eyes of his beloved sister and said, "My dearest sister, you know me well, but you must not deceive yourself. Man is the only living creature who knows he will one day die. Man does not know just when that time may come, but some of us sense when it may be near. Though I may look better, Eleanor, I am not long for this world." He paused and smiled. "I hope to see you again in paradise."

Eleanor said softly, "God loves you and so do I, John." She hastily left the room before breaking into tears.

Early in the year 1866, Bishop John had constant nose bleeding again and declined steadily. On February 7, he fell into a semi-coma; and early on the morning of February 13, 1866, John Bernard Fitzpatrick, Third Bishop of Boston, breathed his last suffering sigh and became one with the ages.

CHAPTER TWENTY-FOUR

Eleanor seemed unable to cope with the death of her brother. Her deep grief was evident, and she visited Bishop Fitzpatrick's grave every day. She said to Tobey, "The Bishop did not live to see the completion of the new Cathedral of the Holy Cross. Promise me, Tobey, that you will see that John is moved from St. Augustine's Cemetery to the cathedral when it is completed."

"If I live so long myself," Tobey said. "I will see to it."

Eleanor walked aimlessly about the house. Tobey would find her in the garden softly crying. She stopped writing her "Alethe" columns, and when she came to the table she picked at her food.

"Why, Tobey? I know I must believe this is the will of God, but why did God take him from us now?"

She looked at her husband. Tobey was unable to think of anything to say except to answer with his life-long adage, "To be Irish is to know that in the end, the world will break your heart."

"It is not the world that has broken my heart," Eleanor said, "It is the loss of John who was always my spiritual support. Without him, my faith in the goodness and love of God is shaken to the core. John was doing so much good in the world. His sense of reason and logic is so needed in the chaos we face now."

Tobey's heart ached to console Eleanor. He called for their twin son John, now an ordained priest, to come for a visit with his mother. They spent many hours praying together.

"Mother, you know Bishop John would want you to have courage and carry on," said the young Father John.

"Yes, I know that," Eleanor said. "I will try."

The youngest of Tobey and Eleanor's children, Leo Paul, was now at Holy Cross College studying also for the priesthood, and he was able to be with his parents some at their very quiet Boston home where they now spent all their time.

Even their daughter Minnie had left. She had gone to the Ursuline Convent in Montreal, but unlike her mother, she would remain there and take her full vows as a nun. Thomas was in Worcester running Tobey's business and Frank's ship was somewhere in the Gulf of Mexico.

Happiness did come to the Boland household when Terry O'Shea and Bridget, their long-time domestic, announced their intention to marry. The wedding was held in the Boland house with Tobey acting as the father of the bride and the ceremony the first wedding preformed by young Father John, who did get the name of the bride right. Now only Hannah remained to do the housekeeping and cooking for Tobey and Eleanor.

The house that once teemed with so much activity and so many children was still and quiet. In the evenings Tobey and Eleanor sat in the parlor by the fireplace. Since there were no longer any children to read to, they read to each other.

One evening Eleanor looked at Tobey and said, "Oh, Tobey, the house is so empty. You're all I have left."

Tobey smiled. "Yes, my dear, but I'm all you had when you started."

"That's true, Tobey, and I love you with all my heart. I have been blessed to have you as a husband and the father of our children. I will always miss my brother John, but my love for him is a totally different kind of love. I got my spiritual strength from him. Now I can't seem to find that again.

"You know, I used to think it was so unreasonable in the old English dramas I studied long ago when characters died of a broken heart. Now I have decided it is entirely possible."

Such talk and Eleanor's actions disturbed Tobey. He urged her to get out of the house. And eventually she did. Eleanor began to visit the poor in Boston and she went to Worcester and helped those families in Shanty Town in whatever ways she could. She found comfort in teaching the children and she tried to train the women in cleanliness and sanitation in an attempt to prevent so much of the sickness which still prevailed there. Some of her efforts were successful, but in spite of her good works, a terrible typhoid epidemic broke out and great numbers of people came down with the disease and many of them died.

"Eleanor, it concerns me when you go into the village now that the typhoid is so widespread," Tobey begged. "It is so highly contagious; you are taking a great chance."

"God will take care of me," Eleanor said. "I have lived a long life. When it is my time to go, I will go. You of all people are aware that death is something we cannot prevent or control; we simply have to face and accept it."

And Eleanor continued her charity and her good works. She survived the epidemic of typhoid as well as outbreaks of other serious illnesses.

In the autumn of 1879, she was preparing some Halloween treats to take to the children of Shanty Town. She caught a cold which grew worse and settled in her chest and lungs and confined her to bed.

On October 31, Halloween day, she was unable to get up and go to the planned Halloween activity. Tobey sat by her bedside and read to her. Eleanor turned to him and said,

"Please read to me from the Psalms."

Tobey rose and crossed the room and picked up Eleanor's well worn Bible from the table. He sat back down by the bed and opened the book and looked through the pages. Then he began to read.

Praise the Lord O my soul; while I live will I praise the Lord; yea as long as I have any being, I will sing praises unto my God.
O put not your trust in princes nor in any child of man; for there is no help in them.
For when the breath of man goeth forth, he shall turn again to his earth, and then all his thoughts perish.
Blessed is he that hath the God of Jacob for his help, and whose hope is in the Lord his God.
Who made heaven and earth, the sea, and all that therein is; who keepeth his promise forever.

Tobey looked over at Eleanor and saw that her eyes were closed. She is finally sleeping, he thought, and closed the Bible and watched her.

Suddenly Eleanor sat upright and called out, "John, wait for me, I'm coming."

As she fell back on the pillow, a great dread came over Tobey. He took her wrist and felt for a pulse, but he could find none.

Tobey put his head on Eleanor's shoulder and wept. He knew that the angel of death had visited him once more.

CHAPTER TWENTY-FIVE

Time stopped for Tobey when Eleanor died. Everything was dated either before her death or after. Nothing in life seemed to have any meaning for him. He wondered why he was still living when so many of his loved ones had died and were gone forever.

But still the bell tolled. Twin John the priest was not as fortunate as his mother. He contracted a fatal illness while working with the poor Irishmen in their crowded and unhealthy conditions and in1881, only three years after the death of his mother, John, at the age of 38, died from cholera.

Tobey's youngest son, Leo Paul, returned from France where he had been ordained to the priesthood in Aix, and was assigned to the nearly completed new Cathedral of the Holy Cross in Boston. Concerned with his father being alone now, he urged him to accept the invitation of his friend Patrick Denvir and move into the Denvir household where he could have people care for him and see to his needs.

Tobey could no longer abide being in the empty house so he agreed to move to the home of his friend.

Tobey's health was failing and he spent much of the time in bed. Father Leo came to see him almost every day and brought Holy Communion.

One evening Tobey asked Leo to sit with him awhile longer.

"Son," he said, "I want you to know that I am at peace with God, and I am ready to join those whom I love who have gone before me. I have had a long life filled with many accomplishments. I have built canals, railroads, churches, buildings and a college. I have loved two women who blessed my life. I have buried my babies and my grown sons, and I have seen three of my children go into the service of the church. I have no regrets.

"I am thankful that you, my own son, are here to give me my last rites. Do not grieve for me. It is time for me to go. And so goodbye."

On Monday, September 3, 1883, Tobias Francis Boland, the great Irish Pioneer, quietly slipped into the life hereafter.

Taken from the newspaper *The Boston Pilot*, September 3, 1883

TOBIAS FRANCIS BOLAND

On Monday, September 3, 1883, a venerable and honored layman of the Archdiocese of Boston, died at the residence of his life-long friend, Patrick Denvir, in Charlestown District. Four score years filed up the measure of his life. Born in Tipperary, Ireland, the deceased sought our shores when but yet a young man in 1825. Mr. Boland married twice, first to Miss Mary Ellen McCauley of Washington, D. C. On the demise of his first wife, Mr. Boland married Miss Eleanor Fitzpatrick, sister of the late lamented Rt. Rev. J.B. Fitzpatrick, third Bishop of Boston.

The oldest readers of the PILOT and its predecessor, The JESUIT, will fondly remember Miss Fitzpatrick for the many beautiful contributions of her pen to the columns of either paper, over the nom de plume of Alethe.

Of the children begotten to his marriages, the sole survivors are Thomas Boland of Worcester and the Rev. Leo Paul Boland, rector at The Cathedral of the Holy Cross.

When Mr. Boland went to Worcester, there were eighteen Catholic families in the city which now has a Catholic population of some 30,000. During a busy life of half a century as contractor and builder, with headquarters in Boston and Worcester, the subject of our sketch superintended the erection of Holy Cross College, Worcester; St. Mary's Church (the oldest church now in use in the Boston Diocese), St John's in Worcester and churches of Taunton, Watertown, and other towns. During the administration of President Pierce, Mr. Boland served faithfully as a custom house inspector, and thereafter retired to private life to enjoy a well earned competency. During the career of the deceased, he made the cause of religion, albeit unostentatiously, many and generous donations. Notable among these stand the beautiful altar of the Blessed Virgin and the grand memorial window perpetuating his own and the names of his beloved spouses will ever claim from devout worshipers at the Cathedral a prayer of fond remembrance. During his last illness his great sufferings were marked with a profound religious resignation. His consciousness did not appear to leave him until he gave up his soul to God as he received the last blessing from the hands of his reverend son,

Father Boland of the Cathedral. In his will Mr. Boland showed the charitableness in his nature which characterized him through life by bequeathing a sign of money to nearly every Catholic institution in Boston. As he lived, so he died with malice towards none, without an enemy, with countless friends who he loved.

May Eternal rest grant him, Oh Lord, and perpetual life be shown unto him.

To be Irish is to know that in the end,

the world will break your heart.

Other Books by These Authors

Margaret Boland Ellis

Be Good Sweet Maid
Golden Memories of Navy Blue

A Brief Garland

Manifold Sins

The Shamrock Diary
(Writing as Megan O'Meara)

A Wind Called Frederic

Thomas L. Rooney

Tobey Boland and the Blackstone Canal
(Story for Children)

The Years of the Great Depression

ABOUT THE AUTHORS

Margaret Boland Ellis is the great granddaughter of Tobias Boland and the only living descendent of the Irish Pioneer in her generation. She was born in Meridian, Mississippi and although she has had a long career in education, athletics, and public relations, her primary occupation has always been writing. She presently lives on the Gulf Coast.

Thomas L. Rooney is a native of Massachusetts. Except for service in the military, he has always lived in New England. His mother was born in Ireland, and he is very active in the Irish community around Worcester and Boston.
A retired banker, he now spends his time doing historical research and presenting programs to schools and clubs. He lives in Shrewsbury, Massachusetts.